# IRISH TRADITIONAL MUSIC

CIARÁN CARSON

First published and printed by
The Appletree Press Ltd
7 James Street South
Belfast BT2 8DL
1986

© Ciarán Carson, 1986

All rights reserved

British Library Cataloguing in Publication Data
Carson, Ciarán
  Irish traditional music.
  1. Folk music—Ireland
  I. Title
  781.7415      ML3654

ISBN 0-86281-168-6

9 8 7 6 5 4 3 2 1

# Acknowledgements

Acknowledgements are made to the following: to MacMillan, Inc. for the quotation from *Baroque Music: A Practical Guide for the Performer* by Victor Rangel-Ribeiro (Copyright © 1981 by Schirmer Books, a Division of MacMillan, Inc. Reprinted by permission of the publisher); to the Dolmen Press Ltd for the quotation from 'Suggested Links Between Eastern and Celtic Music' by Fanny Feehan in *The Celtic Consciousness* edited by Robert O'Driscoll (The Dolmen Press, 1982); to the authors and The Blackstaff Press Ltd for extracts from *The Northern Fiddler* by Allen Feldman and Eamon O'Doherty (The Blackstaff Press, 1979); to The Blackstaff Press and the author for quotations from *Shamrock, Rose and Thistle* by Hugh Shields (The Blackstaff Press, 1981).

# Contents

| | |
|---|---|
| What is Traditional Music? | 5 |
| How Irish is Irish Traditional Music? | 5 |
| Some General Notions about the Music | 6 |
| The Instruments | 11 |
| The Uilleann Pipes | 12 |
| The Fiddle | 17 |
| The Flute | 25 |
| The Tin Whistle | 29 |
| Free-reed Instruments | 31 |
| The Harp | 35 |
| The Bodhrán | 37 |
| Other Instruments | 39 |
| Dancing and Music | 41 |
| The Song Tradition | 45 |
| Recent Developments | 51 |
| Etiquette | 55 |
| Technical Supplement | 59 |
| Where It's At | 63 |
| Selected Bibliography | 67 |
| Ten Recommended Records | 70 |

*There are three ways of telling every story
but a thousand ways of singing every song*
                                      Irish proverb

*A little nonsense now and then
Is often relished by the best of men*
                                      Irish proverb

# What is Traditional Music?

Irish traditional music accords to a definition made by the International Folk Music Council in 1954:

> Folk music is the product of a musical tradition that has been evolved through the process of oral transmission. The factors that shape the tradition are: (i) continuity which links the present with the past; (ii) variation which springs from the individual or the group; (iii) selection by the community, which determines the form or forms in which the music survives.

In Ireland, a distinction is made between 'traditional' and 'folk' music , 'folk' music having a wider and sometimes pejorative interpretation; it can refer to 'contemporary' songs with guitar accompaniment, for example. Since traditional musicians call the music traditional music, we might as well call it that too.

Traditional music comprises two broad categories; instrumental music, which is mostly dance music (reels, jigs, hornpipes, polkas, and the like), and the song tradition, which is mostly unaccompanied solo singing.

# How Irish is Irish Traditional Music?

It is Irish by virtue of its being played in the island called Ireland.

There is a general feel to this music which distinguishes it from the traditional music, of, say, Scotland, or the Eastern United States. But there are many similarities between Irish traditional music and the traditional music of Scotland and the Eastern United States.

There are many differences within Irish traditional music: the music of West Cork is different from the music of Donegal. Perhaps we can see them as dialects of a language: a musician from Donegal will find it difficult to play with a musician from West Cork; he might find it equally difficult to understand his accent.

One of the features of traditional music is its capacity for absorption, retention and change. Traditional music has always drawn on many influences and sources: for example, the ballroom schottisches and polkas of polite 19th-century society, English music-hall songs, Scottish bagpipe music, and even the music of visiting blackface minstrel troupes. The trend continues to the present day – there is a current fashion for making traditional dance tunes from such commonplace material as the theme tune to 'Dallas'. The traditional group De Danann have made a hornpipe from the Beatles' song 'Hey Jude'. Whether or not these tunes survive in the future will be determined by the community, in this case other traditional musicians and their audience.

In this context, 'Irish' means absorbing other influences and making them feel at home.

## Some General Notions about the Music

Tradition implies continuity, the creation of new music within an established framework. That framework is a musical language. In order to speak the language, one must know its grammar, its syntax, its way of saying things. This language is learned, like other languages, by listening, by imitation, by engaging in a social discourse.

The language of traditional music is not the language of classical music. There may, however, be some parallels between traditional music and Baroque music. Consider the following quotations:

> In those rare cases where a Baroque composer wrote a melodic line that he did not wish anybody to ornament or elaborate, he usually wrote a cautionary note, such as *come sta (as is* or *play as written)*. But where the melodic line is spare, simple and carries no cautionary notice, almost invariably the performer was expected to elaborate it. The composer in effect set up a very sketchy outline – a roadmap, shall we say, showing points from A to B; the musical traveller was expected to pick his own route. In a single measure, it is the music equivalent of saying to a friend, 'I don't care what you do at the Place de la Concorde, but meet me on the third level of the Eiffel Tower at 4 p.m.' In an entire composition, it is like journeying from New York to San Francisco: the twentieth-century musician-motorist takes the superhighway as being the shortest distance between two given points; the true Baroque musician would take the scenic route, putting in all manner of little side trips along the way. The variations would be endless. It would then be possible to go from New York to San Francisco a thousand times over, never covering exactly the same ground twice, and discovering fresh delights each time.
>
> Victor Rangel-Ribeiro *Baroque Music*

> I shall . . . state here, as a result of my own experience as a collector of our melodies, that I rarely, if ever, obtained two settings of an unpublished air that were strictly the same; though in some instances, I have gotten as many as fifty notations of the one melody. In many instances, indeed, I have found the difference between one version and another to have been so great, that it was only by a careful analysis of their structure, aided perhaps by a knowledge of their history and the progress of their mutations, that they could be recognised as being essentially the same air.
>
> George Petrie *Collection of the Ancient Music of Ireland*

Variation, then, is a principle of traditional music.

The same tune is never the same tune twice. A traditional tune printed in a book is not *the* tune; it is a description of one of its many possible shapes.

The same tune played by the same musician on different occasions will not be the same tune.

The same tune may have many different names.

The tune all depends.

> The sound of the atmosphere, the weather, changed my style. But I could hear, since me being an air-music man. The air came in different, with a different sound of music. Well, the atmosphere, when the wind blowing carries music along. I don't know if it affects you or not, but it's a sounding that's in the air, you see? And I don't know where it comes from – it could come from the airplanes, or the moaning of automobiles, but anyway it leaves an air current in the air, you see. That gets in the wind, makes a sounding, you know? All that sounding works up to a blues.
> Robert Pete Williams, blues guitarist

The tune depends on what happens. You can see this in the names of some tunes. These names are labels, gestures, chance encounters between music and an off-hand comment. An incident might recall a tune; a snippet of talk might become a formal title, for want of a better name: 'When You're Sick, Is It Tay You Want'; 'The Trip to the Jacks'; 'Don't Bother Me'; 'How Much Have You Got'; 'The Day We Paid the Rent'; 'You're a Long Time Courting'; 'The Fiddler is Drunk'; 'One Before We Go'; 'Hush the Cat from under the Table'.

All this is a roundabout way to talking about what actually happens. The music is concerned with conversation, crack, diversion, passing the time. It is about being in one place at one time, and remembering all the other times. Maybe traditional music is contemporary music:

> When we separate music from life what we get is art (a compendium of masterpieces). With contemporary music, when it is actually contemporary, we have no time to make that separation (which protects us from living) and so contemporary music is not so much art as it is life and anyone making it no sooner finishes one of it than he

> begins making another just as people keep on washing dishes, brushing their teeth, getting sleepy, and so on.
>
> John Cage

Because of this it is difficult to say if a traditional musician has a repertoire. The tunes he plays are the tunes he plays at any given time. He will learn new tunes and forget others. He might find himself liking what he thinks is a new tune which the other musician learned from him years ago. In that time maybe it has become a new tune: the same tune is never the same tune twice. He might only play certain tunes with certain people. The music is a language: sometimes a private language, though others can read their own meaning into it.

Because of this it is difficult to say if traditional music has performances, if by *performance* we mean a concert programme. Since the music can happen anywhere, or at any time, it often does. It can happen in a sheugh, behind a haystack, in an alleyway, in a bungalow, in a parish hall, in a pub, on a street corner. There is no definite beginning, and no definite end. This is not to say that there are no rules. The rules are just different. They are a bit like the rules of conversation. The programme, what is talked about, will change according to who is there, and where they are, and whoever might be listening.

At the same time every individual tune – reel, jig, hornpipe or whatever – has a very definite beginning and end. The musician does what he is doing within sixteen bars, and then he does it again, only differently. There are very definite unspoken rules. How does one learn them?

> There is only one way of becoming a traditional player or singer, and that is by listening to genuine material performed in a traditional manner.
>
> Breandán Breathnach, *Folk Music and Dances of Ireland*

This should be obvious, but you would be surprised at the number of non-traditional musicians who try to learn traditional music from a book.

The language of traditional music is not the language of classical music. Since no Received Pronunciation exists in traditional music, it is difficult to generalise about its various accents. But the following generalisations are true of most traditional musicians:

**Traditional Music**

*Fiddle*
No use of vibrato; tone relaxed rather than brilliant; a full bow is rarely used; changes of bow are accentuated; playing is only in the first position.

*Flute*
The tone is woody or even hoarse; breathing is often deliberately accentuated; there is a two-octave range.

*Singing*
No vibrato; no dynamic or dramatic effects; little use of facial expression; 'head' voice, sometimes nasalised; the song will end in a casual throwaway manner.

**Classical Music**

*Violin*
Vibrato is an integral part of technique; the tone is brilliant and powerful; the bow is 'seamless' and changes of direction are only accentuated for special effect; playing is in all positions.

*Flute*
The tone is metallic and clean; the ideal way to breathe is to appear not to breathe at all; there is a three-octave range.

*Singing*
Vibrato; dynamic and dramatic effects; sentiments of the song emphasised by facial expression; 'chest' voice with no nasalisation; the song will end with a flourish.

It is also generally true that the concepts of crescendo and diminuendo are utterly foreign to traditional music.

I have heard classically-minded musicians and listeners complain that traditional musicians do not exploit the full potential of their instrument. This is a misapprehension. The instrument is only a means towards an end. One might as well complain that the sonnet form in poetry is limited because it has only fourteen lines. Conversely, the classical musician, especially when he attempts to play traditional music, can sound exaggerated, histrionic and vulgar to the traditional musician.

It follows that any classical training on an instrument is likely to be an impediment to the traditional musician.

## The Instruments

There is no such thing as a traditional instrument. An instrument is only a means towards an end; in this case, the production of traditional music. Whether or not the musician produces music that is traditional is a matter between himself, his instrument, and the world at large.

Some instruments may suit traditional music better than others. The simple-system flute, for example. But it is unlikely that a classical musician would produce traditional music on the simple-system flute.

I once heard great traditional music being played by a saxophone and accordion duet. Among the other instruments which have accommodated traditional music, more or less successfully, are the jew's harp, the mouth-organ, the tenor banjo, the 5-string banjo, the banjo-mandoline, the mandoline, the fiddle, the bouzouki, the szaz, the ivy leaf, the tin whistle, the concertina, the piano accordion, the button accordion, the melodeon, the harp, the hammer dulcimer, the clavichord, the harpsichord, the mandola, the viola, the guitar and the Moog synthesizer.

I have never heard Irish traditional music being played on the clarinet. I don't know why this should be. Nor the euphonium, though I can understand why this might be. I have never heard Irish traditional music being played on the trombone. Nor the trumpet. These instruments are used in traditional jazz. That they are not used in traditional Irish music suggests two different usages of the word 'traditional'.

## The Uilleann Pipes

The uilleann pipes (pronounced, as near as English orthography allows, 'illyun' – not 'yooleeun' as many would have it) are an Irish development of an instrument which is found in many versions throughout the world: Groves' *Dictionary of Musical Instruments* lists seventy different types of bagpipe. The uilleann pipes are generally thought to have evolved from the old Irish war-pipes (which were somewhat similar to the Scottish pipes) about the beginning of the 18th century. Their distinguishing characteristics are: a bag filled by a bellows, not a blow pipe; a chanter or melody pipe which gives a two-octave range; and the addition of regulators which can be used for accompanying the melody. The present full set of pipes comprises bag, bellows, chanter, drones and regulators.

Though the correct name for the instrument is held by some authorities to be 'union' pipes – referring to the union of chanter and regulators – the term 'uilleann pipes' (meaning elbow pipes) is in such general usage that it would be pedantic to object to it.

The modern uilleann pipes, pitched in D or sometimes E flat, were developed in Philadelphia in the latter half of the 19th century by the Taylor brothers, who emigrated from Drogheda. Previously, the pipes could be pitched in anything from around B flat to C sharp; the Taylor pipes were in a way a product of market forces, since they produced the greater volume needed to fill the American concert and music halls, where Irish music was a flourishing industry. Many aficionados of the pipes prefer the comparatively mellow, restrained tone of the old flat sets; significantly, many younger pipers are returning to these instruments – yet another illustration of Irish traditional music as the snake biting its own tail.

The pipes are in many ways a curious hybrid: since Irish music is essentially melodic, it might be thought that the regulators, which permit harmonic accompaniment, are unnecessary. A possible explanation for their presence is afforded by O'Farrell (first name unknown) who published a treatise on the pipes around 1797-1800. This is the title page:

O'Farrell's 'playing... in the Favourite Pantomime of Oscar and Malvina' is of some significance. Irish pipers, according to Francis O'Neill *(Irish Minstrels and Musicians)*, were no rarity on the London stage; and it is evident that they were not playing exclusively Irish music. O'Farrell's treatise, in fact, gives fingering charts for a fully chromatic scale; and, since fully-keyed chromatic chanters from the period exist, we can infer that they must have been used to play music other than Irish traditional music, which very rarely uses accidentals. Harmonic accompaniment would have been perfectly appropriate to the music of popular pantomime and opera: hence the regulators. It is also a matter of historical record that the pipes were a favourite instrument of the Anglo-Irish gentry. O'Neill's *Irish Minstrels and Musicians* devotes a whole chapter to 'Gentlemen Pipers', noting that George II was so much delighted with the performance of an Irish gentleman on the bagpipe that he ordered a medal to be struck for him. Presumably many such gentlemen, given their predeliction for playing before royalty, would aspire to musical tastes somewhat more refined than those of the peasantry. Were the pipes, then, an instrument of the people, or a plaything of a wealthy leisured class? (Lord Rossmore, one of these gentlemen, owned some 15,000 acres of Co. Monaghan.) Certainly, it is doubtful if the man in the street or the man in the bog could afford some of the instruments which have passed down from the time: these were elaborately-crafted productions using the most expensive materials – exotic woods, ivory and silver. On the other hand, there is some evidence to suggest that pipes were made from local materials such as boortree. Whatever the case, the regulators, thought by many to be an integral component of the uilleann pipes, seem to have been grafted on (is it accidental that they are inserted into that part of the pipes known as the *stock*?) to accommodate non-Irish music. Their role remains problematic to this day, and some authorities maintain that they should be dispensed with altogether. Certainly, the kind of vamping accompaniment which is possible on the regulators is often a hindrance to the music: as the late Seamus Ennis put it, 'the regulators are an abomination if they are used as a monotonous percussion'. Many pipers use the regulators for occasional rhythmic emphasis, in keeping with the spirit of the music; others succumb to the temptation to make as much use as possible of an expensive and burdensome appendage. For whatever reason, most pipers want to have a full set of pipes, though they may never exploit their whole harmonic range; it seems to be a rule of the club, where a gentleman dare not be seen in public without his regulators.

> An Irish-American writer named Barry, speaking of the modern Irish bagpipes, says, 'In its original form it had nothing like the range of capabilities which now enables Mr Bohan to perform on it not only the "Humors of Ballinahinch", "Shaun O'Dheir an Gleanna", "Paddy O'Carroll", "The Fox Chase" and "The Blackbird", but serious productions such as Corentina's song from *Dinorah* and Bach's *Pastorale* in F major'.... A Dublin correspondent adds, 'In the use of the regulators, Bohan was far ahead of all other players of his day.... In his old age, the minstrel was evidently far from prosperous, and he was indebted for many favours to the generous John Hingston, steward of Trinity College. The latter, who was Canon Goodman's particular friend, fitted him out with a presentable suit of clothing and played in concert with him at the Viceregal Lodge before the Prince of Wales, afterwards King Edward VII.
>
> Francis O'Neill
> *Irish Minstrels and Musicians*

It is perhaps ironic, given their history, that the pipes should be regarded in many quarters as *the* quintessentially Irish instrument; there is, indeed, a school of thought which holds that all Irish traditional instrumental music should aspire to the condition of the pipes, and that any form of decoration or ornamentation is illegitimate unless it can be done on the pipes.

This, of course, is a matter of taste and prejudice; but it has to be admitted that, for those who seek to embody the spirit of the nation in a physical object, the pipes are an ideal hobby-horse. They are thingy, complicated; they are a conversation-piece. Reeds, regulators, drones, comparative length of chanters, beeswax, drones, hemp, rushes, pads, popping pads, valves, drones, can be discussed until the cows come home.

According to the late Seamus Ennis (one of the greatest pipers of modern times) there are three styles of piping: the 'real close fingering of the North'; 'loose or open fingering' and the 'normal or Drawing Room style' (from an interview in *Treoir* vol. 5, no. 2). He goes on to say, 'There are far too many pipers

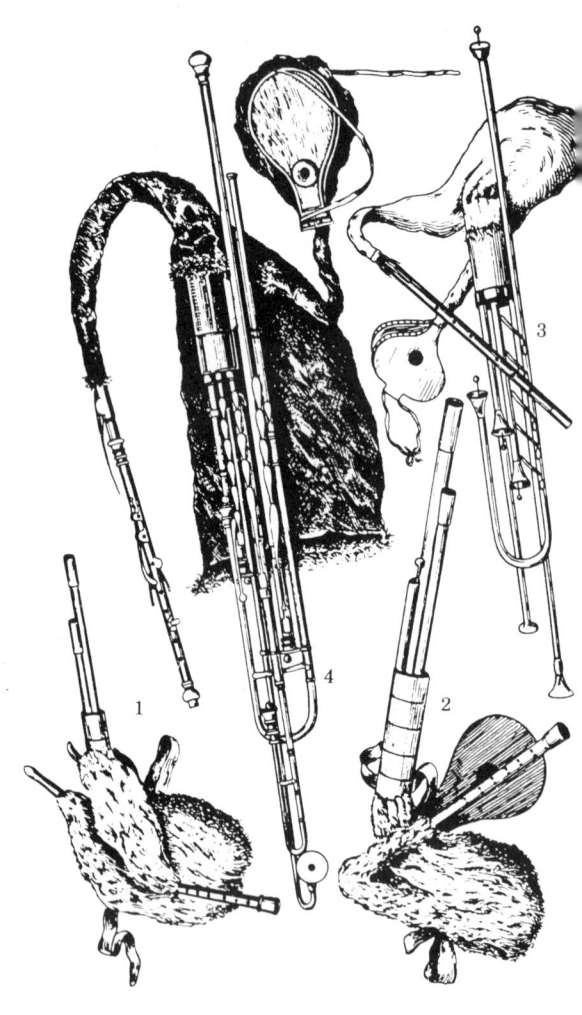

1. *Ancient Irish Bagpipe*
2. *Cuislean or Bellows Pipes*
3. *Primitive Union Pipes*
4. *Egan's Improved Union Pipes*

today who think they have it and they haven't even started yet. Tradition has it that it takes 7 years practising and 7 years playing to make a piper. After 21 years I wasn't as able as I am now and if my father were alive today I would still be learning from him.' Interestingly, Ennis gives fingerings for E and F sharp in the third octave – notes that may have been useful for playing some 'Drawing Room' pieces, but which never occur in traditional music, though maybe Ennis, being Ennis, occasionally threw them in just to show they could be done. Showmanship seems to be a trait in some pipers: Finbarr Furey, asked why he played so fast, is supposed to have replied, 'Because I can.'

Until comparatively recently the pipes seemed in danger of extinction; however, organisations such as Na Píobairí Uilleann, formed in 1968 under the chairmanship of the late Breandán Breathnach, have helped to ensure their survival, and there are probably more pipers now than in any time in history, though perhaps, if we are to take Ennis at face value, many of them may not have even started yet.

> **píobaire,** a piper; a kind of eel; **píobaire fraoigh,** a grasshopper.
>
> **uille,** an elbow, anything resembling an elbow, an angle, a structural knee or elbow, a knee-timber, the elbow or base angle of a spear-head, the angle of a shield, a corner or a nook, an inclination; poverty.
>
> Rev. Patrick S. Dinneen
> *An Irish-English Dictionary*

## The Fiddle

In contemporary usage, the fiddle is a violin, considered as a purely physical object; the two words are, in fact, etymologically related. The orchestral player usually refers to himself (perhaps jocularly) as a fiddle-player; the traditional musician will call him a violin-player. This useful distinction will be preserved here.

Historically, the term 'fiddle' is a generic term for 'any chordophone of the lute family played with a bow' (Groves' *Dictionary of Musical Instruments*) and it is interesting to note that there is some evidence to suppose that an instrument of this type, a precursor of the modern violin, was played in Ireland:

> When the fiddle first came to Donegal, it wasn't the flat ones that's in it now, you know. In that time, there were fiddles that had a stoop to the neck, you see, the neck was sort of bent. They used to call them the crooked-necked fiddle. They called it in Irish *an fhideal cham*. . . . they kept at these till these (violins) came across the water from Scotland. . . .
>
> Mickey Byrne, quoted in<br/>Feldman and O'Doherty<br/>*The Northern Fiddler*

The difference between a fiddle and a violin is a difference of attitude and technique.

Since all traditional music can be played in the first position, the modern classical hold is not necessary: the fiddle may be held against the chest, shoulder or upper arm, with the neck resting against the palm of the hand, more or less supporting the instrument. The production of vibrato is difficult in such a position, which is just as well, since vibrato is inappropriate to traditional music. In recent years, however, these mannerisms have been observed to shift towards classical violin technique: Eithne and Brian Vallely, for instance, in their book *Learn to Play the Fiddle* recommend the classical hold 'simply because it is the easiest for a beginner and gives more control'. If traditional music results from this method, well and good; the end can justify the means. However, vibrato has been making some incursions into traditional music, notably in slow air playing. Perhaps this is a question of mere technique; perhaps it is a question of the all-too-prevalent attitude that such technique has a social and aesthetic imprimatur denied to the traditional musician.

Similarly, a wide range of bow grips can be observed: the stick may be held about a third of the way out from the frog with the thumb straight or bent backwards, or even with the thumb held under the hair; or the grip may approach that of classical technique. Some styles of traditional playing use a very short, vigorous bow-stroke; others may use a comparatively long bow. Adjudicators in fiddle competitions have tended to criticise competitors for not using the full length of the bow: this is a misapprehension disseminated by secondary school teachers who think that one technique is universally applicable to all forms of music.

Again, the violin-player's notion of good tone is inappropriate to fiddle-playing; indeed, the manner in which it is produced may mitigate against good traditional playing, which never employs dynamic effects.

Other characteristics which distinguish the fiddle from the violin are: personal variations in the tension of the bow, some preferring a very slack bow, others a very tight one; occasional use of non-standard tunings, such as a-e' -a' e", or tuning considerably below or above concert pitch; and variations in the height and contour of the bridge. The widespread habit of leaving rosin to accumulate under the bridge may not be simply a matter of laziness and lack of personal hygiene, but an active decision which results in a thinner, more nasal tone.

Traditional fiddle-players generally use steel strings.

Regional fiddle styles can still be distinguished, ranging from the short staccato bowing of Donegal to the longer, more relaxed bowing of Kerry. Younger musicians, however, will tend to play in an eclectic style based on Sligo fiddle-playing, though there are many exceptions to the rule – notably in the North, where some younger players have consciously adopted a Donegal style.

Unquestionably, the greatest influence on fiddle-playing in this century has been the 78 rpm recordings of Michael Coleman, made in the USA in the twenties and thirties, and now still widely available on several LP compilations. Coleman's deification is examined below:

In 1903 Francis O'Neill, General Superintendent of the Chicago Police, published his *Music of Ireland – Eighteen Hundred and Fifty Melodies: Airs, Jigs, Reels, Hornpipes, Long Dances, Marches, etc., Many of which are now Published for the First Time, Collected from all Available Sources.* O'Neill was a traditional flute-player from West Cork who had run away to sea, been shipwrecked and, after his rescue and arrival in the New World, had worked at various jobs including those of cowboy and schoolteacher before his enlistment in the police force. 'The Book', as it became known to traditional musicians, was compiled in his spare time: tunes were noted down from memory, from printed sources, but mostly from the playing of Irish musicians in the Chicago area, many of whom O'Neill had recruited to the force. One of the Book's virtues is its eclecticism: it reflected the various styles and repertoires of a wide range of Irish emigré musicians. It suggests that music comes from circumstances, from the actual, from personal encounter. While there are many transcriptional errors, unlikely key signatures, and some tunes duplicated in slightly different versions, these do not matter greatly. The traditional musician will make the necessary transcriptional corrections almost without thinking; and having several different versions of one tune is, if anything, an advantage. Traditional music, in the real world, does not conform to any one stylistic impulse; if it can be thought of as a musical language, it contains many different dialects, idiolects, and accents, and O'Neill's magpie instincts recognised this.

In 1976 the American musicologist Miles Krassen published 'a newly printed and corrected' version of

O'Neill. It is interesting to note that his corrections go far beyond the alterations of accidentals and key signatures; Krassen's concern is to impose a stylistic uniformity on the book, as he states in his preface:

> O'Neill's work was completed long before the golden age of Irish recordings. Consequently he had little access to the Sligo fiddle music which has exerted so major an influence on Irish music over the last fifty years. Since O'Neill's time the recordings of Michael Coleman, in particular, have provided standard settings and stylistic models for players on almost every instrument. Wherever possible the editor has chosen the Coleman setting for inclusion in this work.

Krassen's procedure is, in fact, almost classical in its pursuit of the ideal; music comes from without, instead of within. It is not difficult to see why he has chosen Coleman as his exemplar; at the time the recordings were issued, in the twenties, they had a devastating effect on traditional music, particularly in Ireland. Many fiddle-players tried to imitate Coleman's dazzling technique; some gave up altogether. Because Coleman's music come from outside, because it had received the imprimatur of a prestigious record company, it was seen as definitive and authoritative – all the more so, perhaps, when Coleman's repertory of rolls, triplets, and melodic variations stood out in contrast to the plainer styles of, say, Tyrone and Fermanagh. A musician's notion of what he was doing, until then confined to the local, the personal, the parish, now underwent a crisis of identity. One cannot help but recall Patrick Kavanagh's distinction between the parochial and the provincial, where the provincial implies the adoption of received standards, and parochialism is truth. To this day there are many Irish musicians playing in 'the Coleman style', with varying degrees of success – if they *are* successful, one suspects it is because they have adopted the techniques to their own ends, and are doing something of their own.

It is not too fanciful to suggest that Coleman's adoption by an Irish audience (so much so that the gramophone sometimes replaced the local fiddle-player at house dances) represented something more than musical taste. America in the twenties was paved with gold; it was the land of opportunity; to make it in America was to make it in the world. America was where things happened, like recording contracts and big money (though in reality Coleman and his peers made very little from the business). Ownership of a gramophone was itself a mark of economic status – representing a link with the New World, it was often quite literally 'money from America'. In the words of the song, 'thousands are sailing to America'. Sometimes they sailed in their imagination.

In recent visits to the USA I have caught some glimpses of a mirror image of Ireland in the twenties; now it is young American musicians, often without any discernible Irish ancestry, who are turning to Ireland as a source for their music. Ireland is their America, representing not economic status, but cultural status, an escape from the American dream into a vision of poetic simplicity and celtic spirals. The records of the Roscommon flute-player Matt Molloy, who has played with the Bothy Band, Planxty, and latterly with the Chieftains, have been particularly influential. Any flute-player from America under the age of thirty will in all probability play in a Matt Molloy-ish style (and to be fair, the phenomenon is not unknown in Ireland). It is not difficult to see why. Firstly, the records are available; they have the imprimatur of current folk fashion. Secondly, the aspiring musician can recognise that something very impressive, in a technical sense, is happening: the music can be reduced, like Coleman's, to a catalogue of rolls, cranns, triplets – ignoring, perhaps, the notion that these devices are only a means to an end. Technique, after all, is never inimitable: given a modicum of talent and lots of hard work, similar effects can be achieved. The possibility that better music can be made with less technique has, as yet, not occurred to many young musicians.

Nor does it appear to have occurred to Miles Krassen. His implication that one style of traditional music should be imitated at the expense of others is dangerous and limiting; it runs contrary to the spirit of the thing. How different to O'Neill's approach, as he relates in his *Irish Folk Music – A Fascinating Hobby:*

> Residence in a large cosmopolitan city like Chicago affords opportunities in various lines of investigation and study not possible in other localities. Within the city limits, a territory comprising about two hundred square miles, exiles from all of Ireland's thirty-two counties can be

found. Students in pursuit of any special line of enquiry will find but little difficulty in locating people whose friendship and acquaintance they desire to cultivate. Among Irish and Scotch music lovers, every new arrival having musical taste or talent is welcomed and introduced to the 'Craft', to the mutual advantage of all concerned, and there is as much rejoicing on the discovery of a new expert as there is among astronomers on the announcement of a new asteroid or comet.

O'Neill was fortunate in having access to such diversity. Yet so do we, through the media of the tape-recorder, the record, the radio. They should be used not to institutionalise the music, to establish a Received Pronunciation, but to record and explore its dialects, its moments of personal and intimate beauty, and return them to a living tradition.

*Belfast Review*

### *You Learn Something New Every Day*

Willie Corrigan was a great fiddle player.
The talk of the country.
And if anything was going,
Or any Yankees home or going away,
Willie Corrigan was sent for.
There was no other fiddler like Willie
    Corrigan.

But there came a tramp boy
    round the country one time,
and he come and he was looking
    to stop overnight.
And one thing and another.
And he came into Corrigan's – Corrigan was
    living on his lone –
and he came into Corrigan's and he talked to
    Corrigan
and he got a bowl of tea or whatever
    and a bit of bread
or whatever he had from Corrigan.

And he asked could he get staying
    for a lock of days
that his feet were sore walking the roads
and could he get staying a while.

Corrigan says,
I haven't much for ye to do now

at this time of year.
But he says,
Sure if ye want to do any wee bits of jobs
I'll keep you for a week or a fortnight anyway.
Well, the man says, that'll be grand,
even if it was only scuffling round
or some wee job, just that I'd rest myself
that I'd be out on the road again.
Well, says Corrigan, All right, you're
    welcome to stay.

So every night
when Corrigan would come in at bedtime
after doing bits of things around the house,
    he'd come in
and take down his fiddle off the wall.

And there was a sort of *cuilce* bed
that was built in the wall for lying in there.
I suppose some people would lie in
and keep on the fire all night
and be up early in the morning.
But anyway this boy got this bed

And Willie, ay, Willie was up in the room lying,
it was a room and a kitchen just.
And this boy'd be lying in the ould *cuilce*
resting himself and listening to Willie
playing away at the fiddle every night.

And about a week after he was playing away
this boy was in the bed lying,
maybe smoking a pipe or something
or listening to him.

Anyway, he says to Willie, Willie, he says,
you're playing that tune wrong.

Jesus, Corrigan was offended.
What do you say?
I say, Willie, you're playing that tune wrong,
and another thing,
I don't think ye have that fiddle tuned.
Well, tune her you, says he,
and he fired her into the bed
and he nearly took the head off him with it.
Like, telling Willie Corrigan
that he hadn't the fiddle tuned
that was the top man in the country
nor wasn't playing the tune right.

Well, here you, says he,
and he fired her into the bed
to him across the kitchen

And the boy lifted the fiddle
and he started to tune her up
and Corrigan started listening.

And the boy drew her under his chin,
he sitting himself up in the bed.

I think this is the tune here, Willie, you're at,
and he started to go over the tune.

And Corrigan made across the floor at him
and says he,
And you here this week,
and Jesus,
listening to me scraping the fiddle.
I'll never catch a fiddle again in my life.
And you're playing a tune like that now
that I'm trying to learn all week.

Well, says he,
I just wanted to tell you, Will,
for fear you'd be another week at it.

> from the telling of John Loughran,
> quoted in Feldman and O'Doherty
> *The Northern Fiddler*

## The Flute

The flute most commonly used in Irish traditional music is the so-called 'simple-system' made from a suitable hardwood such as African blackwood, cocus or grenadilla; it is basically a tube closed at one end with six open fingerholes, a mouth-hole (or *embouchure*) and various keys at the side (usually four, six, or eight) to provide accidental notes. These keys are rarely used in traditional music, and, since they are inclined to leak, it is often convenient to tie them down or to dispense with them altogether, plugging the sound-hole with a variety of materials – chewing-gum, plastic wood, Blu-tack, beeswax, etc.; on one occasion, a resourceful flute-player used a large sultana from the fruit-cake provided for the evening's crack – unsuccessfully, as it turned out, for two minutes later it shot out and hit the fiddle-player in the eye. These flutes were the precursors of the modern metal orchestral flute, developed by the German Theobald Boehm in the 1830s and 1840s. They are the cast-offs of polite society, and probably entered traditional music from the back door of the Big House; they are survivors of the vogue for the instrument which swept fashionable Europe at the end of the 18th and beginning of the 19th centuries, and, somewhat later, perhaps, permeated the consciousness of the Anglo-Irish gentry. Fashions changed; wood was superceded by metal, open holes by an elaborate system of levers, springs and pads, and the old flute was taken up by the musicians of 'the Hidden Ireland'. Or so one version of the story goes.

Until recently this type of flute, usually of 19th-century English or German manufacture, could only be obtained by circuitous and devious means: begging, borrowing, stealing, haunting auctions and junk-shops; listening to the grapevine. Now that the second-hand supply has started to dry up, young Irish instrument-makers are producing simple-system flutes based on reliable English makes such as Rudall & Rose or Potter; the old has become the new.

It is perhaps worth pointing out that some type of whistle or flute-like instrument is likely to have existed in Ireland before the introduction of the orchestral flute. Hard evidence for this supposition is not easily come by, but older flute-players in the Sligo-Leitrim area remember people making flutes from such diverse materials as boor-tree, the spokes from cartwheels, and even, in deference to a more up-dated technology, bicycle-pumps.

Old simple-system band flutes pitched in F and B flat (sometimes called fifes) or E flat (sometimes called 'three-quarter' flutes) are also played, mainly for solo music.

It has been said that the inherent characteristics of the simple-system flute are congenial to traditional music; on the other hand, the instrument has modified the music. Whatever the case, traditional players in general prefer it to the Boehm system: the tone of the wooden flute seems more human; the contact of bare fingertips on open holes facilitates ornaments and slides; you can feel the air. Just to confuse things, one of the most highly-regarded players of modern times, the late Paddy Taylor, played a wooden-bodied Boehm-system flute.

Flute-playing is associated especially with the

Sligo-Leitrim- Roscommon area. No-one that I have asked seems to know why, though in comparatively recent times its prevalence might be due to the fact that one of the few flute-players who made commercial recordings in the 1920s was a Leitrim man, John McKenna; his settings of tunes still have a big influence on traditional music today. McKenna emigrated to New York, where he worked in the City Fire Department; his job, apparently, was to arrive at the fire after it had been put out and clear up the debris. It makes a nice metaphor for his style of playing, in which established patterns of phrasing are demolished and then reconstructed, bits and pieces arising out of the wreckage. McKenna's playing is comparatively sparing in the use of rolls; phrases are filled in instead by melodic runs and triplets, and he can suggest a whole world of ornamental and melodic possibility by the alteration of a 'standard' note, or by ignoring the note altogether and taking a breath instead. The breath is what makes McKenna's music: it is deliberately accentuated, unlike classical flute-playing where the aim is a smooth, uncluttered flow. People accustomed to classical playing might therefore think that the technique is deficient; it is, in fact, a very demanding one involving a precise control of the diaphragm and a kind of articulated cough at the back of the throat. The result is a bit like a steam engine. As I heard another flute-player remark affectionately, 'McKenna was only an oul' puffer, but he was a great oul' puffer.' Until recently, McKenna's recordings were not generally available; this situation was rectified, in June 1986, by the issue of an excellent cassette tape of some of his original 78 rpm records, published by the John McKenna Traditional Society, Drumkeerin, Co. Leitrim.


It has already been noted that the supply of second-hand flutes has started to dry up. However, it is still possible to obtain a good English flute, though prices have risen dramatically in recent years. One can expect, for instance, to pay £500 and upwards for a Rudall & Rose in good condition. If you are buying a flute for the first time, find a flute-player with some experience to advise you on the purchase, as what looks good may not play well, and vice versa. It is generally accepted that a good old flute is better than a good new flute; however, the standard of flute-making in Ireland has been rising steadily, and the best of the new instruments compare favourably with the classic English makes.

Flutes, like any other instrument, should never be left in the presence of excessive heat or moisture. Some traditional flute-players might be observed lubricating the bore of their instrument with water, or even stout or whiskey. This is not recommended; you are likely to end up with a cracked flute. If the bore is dry and doesn't respond well to playing, swab it with a little almond oil. Linseed oil is not a good idea, as it builds up a hard deposit in the bore which will affect the tuning of the instrument. One flute-player was known to use the oil from a tin of sardines in an emergency: effective, but nasty.

Every so often, especially if you use a lot of oil, give the flute a good cleaning with a tightly-rolled piece of newspaper. After every playing the flute should be swabbed with a silk handerchief attached to a stick or skewer (a chopstick is ideal for the job).

It must be said that these precautions are often successfully disregarded. One of the best flutes I ever played was an old E flat band flute that had its various cracks bound up with insulating tape and chewing gum; the bore was festooned by years' accumulation of dirt, oil, sputum and fungus. Maybe if it had been cleaned it wouldn't have played so well. Such is the mystery attached to instruments.

### *Out Of The Blue*

I myself began playing when I was very young. One of my earliest memories of music is of a school day when the schoolmaster put eight notes up on the blackboard. Well, he asked me how many notes there were in the scale. I told him there were six. He told me I must be blind, that there were eight notes up there. I was just trying to figure out why he said there were eight when there were only six holes in the tin whistle at home. Then it was very hard to learn music because there was nobody around who knew any notes. Maybe some school teachers knew it, but none of them lived round here then. You had to learn it by ear, on your own, for the most part. 'Twas very hard. I'd be always trying to make tunes out of the blue, play them different than anybody. I myself was more of a music-maker.

Micko Russell (1980)

> I have heard, with much interest, an Irish peasant play... melodies on the flute, although he was quite unacquainted with musical notation – nor did he know the names of the notes on the instrument; yet, he gave those airs, especially the dances, with exact rhythm, and with good tone....
>
> Michael Conran *The National Music of Ireland* (1846)

## The Tin Whistle

The days when the tin whistle was a 'penny whistle' have long since gone, and it is never referred to as such by traditional players. This simple instrument can accommodate many traditional techniques, and it is ideal for the beginner. It is not a toy.

There are two main types of whistle available at the moment: those with a conical bore (the Clarke's whistle, pitched in C) and the cylindrical bore whistle, of which the most common is the 'Generation'. The later is available in the keys of B flat, C, D, E flat, F and G. It is encouraging to note that at long last a whistle of Irish manufacture (*An Fheadóg*, which is Irish for whistle) is available; this compares favourably with the 'Generation' model. It is readily identifiable by its green mouthpiece. In recent years several other types of whistle have appeared, notably the low D whistle, which has a tone not unlike the flute; many people, however, find it difficult to span the very wide spacing of the finger-holes. There are also various hand-crafted wooden whistles, but whatever virtues they might possess should be weighed against their considerable expense (about £40 at 1986 prices).

In recent years the whistle has reached a non-traditional audience through the performances of James Galway, who rather jocosely incorporates it into his stage act. It should be said, however, that his interpretation of 'traditional Irish' tunes would not be regarded as traditional by traditional musicians.

The instrument lends itself to many styles, some of them incorporating uilleann piping and flute technique, but a broad differentiation can be made between staccato and legato playing. Micko Russell of Doolin, Co. Clare, provides an excellent example of the former: his sparse, delicate playing gains its effects by rhythmic starts and stops, emphasised with the tongue, and subtle changes of the melodic contour; typically, he might leave a gap at what would normally be an accented note, and vice versa. Some people regard his inimitable style as overly simple; but this is the art which conceals art. Mary Bergin of Dublin, on the other hand, has an immediately impressive repertory of rolls, cranns, and other ornamentation: the effect is bright, bubbly, elegant; tongueing is used only occasionally to emphasise the basic note of the ornament.

Students of esoterica will be interested to note that some whistle players seem particularly prone to gimmickry: manifestations of the phenomenon include playing with the nose, switching hands in the middle of a tune, and playing two whistles at once (made possible by sealing up the top three holes of one whistle with sellotape). Another impressive parlour trick – though it only works with certain tunes – is to play in D on a C whistle: this is achieved by shifting the hands up one hole and using normal fingering.

It is possible that this sort of behaviour is designed to call attention to an instrument which, even among musicians, has a low profile. Most beginners on the tin whistle see it as a precursor to learning the flute, which it may well be; nevertheless, you can do things on the whistle you can't do on the flute, and perhaps the integrity of the whistle should be more widely recognised. It is an ideal solo instrument, and perhaps its status is a reflection of the current state of the music, where opportunities for solo playing are relatively few.

Though the whistle is a mass-produced object, every whistle is different, and prospective buyers should always ask to try the instrument out in the shop. The contemporary insistence on hygiene can be honoured by the shop stocking a supply of antiseptic swabs.

Whistles can also be customized to suit the individual. A too-shrill 'Generation' whistle can be modified by paring, with a sharp knife, a tiny sliver from the fipple of the plastic mouthpiece. The whole mouthpiece will shift if a lighted match is held underneath it: it can then be moved up or down to flatten or sharpen the fundamental note. This is useful when playing along with an instrument of slightly different pitch to the whistle.

The wooden insert in the mouthpiece of a Clarke's whistle is apt to become unpleasantly soggy with prolonged use, thus affecting the tone. This can be avoided by coating it with a wood sealant. Jim Donoghue, the Sligo whistle player, doctors the wood with a heated hacksaw blade, which seems to give the whistle a very loud, trumpet-like tone.

## Free-reed Instruments

This family of instruments, developed mainly in the latter half of the 19th century, includes the accordion, melodeon, concertina and mouth-organ. The free reed is a metal (usually steel) strip riveted over a slot in a metal frame. A sound is produced when air pressure is applied to the reed.

### The Accordion

The word *accordion* covers a multitude of sins and some virtues. It exists in very many shapes, sizes, forms and tunings, but two broad categories can be

> ...an instrument in harmony with the sentiments of an assassin.
>
> Ambrose Bierce

> ...designed by foreigners for the use of peasants with nether the time, inclination nor application for a worthier instrument...
>
> Seán Ó Riada

> ...an instrument of the people
> Groves' *Dictionary of Music*

> *How do you play the accordion? With a penknife.*
>
> attributed to Christy Moore

distinguished: the button-keyed accordion and the piano accordion. The late Seán Ó Riada disliked both on the grounds that the musician was not in control of the sound he produced – 'he does not make the notes, they are already there, ready to sound at the pressing of a button, produced in an almost entirely mechanical fashion'. Yet the uilleann pipes, considered by many to be *the* traditional instrument, have a similar characteristic: their tone is almost totally dependent on whatever reed the musician happens to be using. Perhaps the real objection to the accordion is that many instruments are badly tuned and that it is relatively easy to produce a slabbery pastiche of traditional music. The piano accordion in particular has many inherent disadvantages: it is heavy and unwieldy; it is often tuned in an inappropriate wide vibrato; its multiplicity of basses provide a constant temptation (often succumbed to) to accompany the melody with inappropriate chords; and, since it is a 'double action' instrument (the same note being sounded on the press and draw of the bellows) it is difficult to provide the articulation necessary for dance music. The speed of the music also means that it is sometimes technically difficult to get from one end of the keyboard to the other without 'playing between the cracks' – that is, accidentally hitting two keys at once, a common fault of many piano accordionists. Recent manifestations of the instrument employ electronic gadgetry to produce a nightmarish version of a *céilí* band, complete with 'drums', 'piano', 'fiddle', 'banjo' and so on. Such developments should, of course, be resisted. Maybe the piano accordion itself is a bad idea, though some players, notably

James Keane, are capable of producing tasteful music on the instrument.

The *button accordion* is a different instrument. Its 'single' action, where two different notes can be sounded on one button by pressing or drawing the bellows, makes for greater articulation and greater economy of fingering. Since the *melodeon* is really an earlier and simpler form of this instrument, it may be appropriate to discuss it first.

The melodeon has ten keys, giving a range of twenty notes over a diatonic scale; two spoon-shaped keys on the left-hand side of the 'box', as it is also known, provide a simple bass. Though the melodeon is a very basic instrument, its very limitations make it suitable in many ways for dance music. Since it is difficult to ornament notes to any great extent, the player is forced to emphasize the rhythm – the basses, in fact, are often used to provide a rhythmic rather than harmonic accompaniment. Interestingly, the very first commercial recording of Irish traditional music, made in 1903, featured the melodeon playing of John J. Kimmel, a New Yorker of German stock who was known as 'The Irish Dutchman'. The immense vitality and drive of Kimmel's music – now available on two LPs – shows what can be achieved on the instrument.

The button accordion developed the melodeon by adding another row of buttons pitched a semi-tone above (or below) the row already available, thus giving a fully chromatic instrument. However, early players of the instrument ignored the chromatic possibilities and treated it much like a melodeon, using the inner row for the melody and only resorting to the outer row for notes unavailable on the inner row (C natural or F natural, for example). It was soon discovered that triplets and rolls could be executed by using the outer button pitched a semitone below the inner button. The success of this technique depends on the speed at which it is done. Chromaticism is foreign to traditional music: however, this kind of roll, when done crisply, will sound as a rhythmic rather than melodic effect; the actual notes will not matter much. This 'press and draw' or 'push and pull' style, as it is known, uses accordions pitched in C/C sharp, C sharp/D and D/D sharp. It is undergoing something of a revival at the moment, mainly due to the influence of Jackie Daly and Martin O'Connor, who prefer it to the other main style of playing, that which uses a B/C accordion.

The B/C accordion is undoubtedly the most popular of this family of instruments. Since it is in some ways technically more difficult to manage – the player has to resort to playing on two rows, or cross-fingering, to play the scale of D – it is perhaps surprising that it was adapted at all for the purposes of traditional music. Maybe it just became available in music shops at the time, and musicians made the best of a bad job. Certainly, at the moment, it is almost impossible to buy anything else other than a B/C accordion in the average music shop. Whatever the case, much of the popularity of the instrument in recent years can be traced to the playing of Paddy O'Brien, who recorded some material in the fifties, and more especially Joe Burke, who is still playing today. Joe Burke is to the B/C box what Michael Coleman was to the fiddle, a player of immense technical resource and imagination who has left a definitive stamp on the music. That he has inspired a host of second-rate imitations is not, of course, his fault. Burke makes a virtue of the technical problems of the instrument, while to other players the technical problems are often just that. The inherent weakness in B/C playing is that less bellows work is involved than on basically one-row systems of playing: this results in a legato effect which diminishes the articulation necessary for dance music.

Other systems which are available include the C/F and the G/D; these are really two-row melodeons, and the latter is very suited to traditional music, though not offering any great facility for rolls.

## The Concertina

As with the accordion, the concertina exists in several systems and tunings. The two basic types are the English concertina, which has single action, and the 'Anglo' or German, which has double action. The most commonly used version in traditional music is the 'Anglo' with the two main rows for each hand tuned in C and G: cross-fingering is thus required for the scale of D.

The advantages of the concertina are that bellows work requires comparatively little effort and that fingering can be achieved without shifting the basic position of the hands; the pleasant tone of the instrument blends well with others, particularly the fiddle.

Concertina-playing, for reasons not fully established, is especially associated with Co. Clare.

## The Mouth Organ

The mouth-organ has a comparatively low profile in traditional music but has been used with great effect by some musicians, notably the Murphy family from Wexford and Eddie Clarke, who has developed a technique of using the slide button on a chromatic mouth-organ to produce rolls.

## The Harp

The harp is responsible for eliciting the first description of Irish instrumental music. In 1183 Giraldus de Barri (or Cambrensis), a Welsh-born Norman priest, visited in Ireland; though he considered the natives 'barbarians' for their general laziness and odd demeanour, he was impressed by their musical ability:

> I find among these people commendable diligence only on musical instruments, on which they are incomparably more skilled than any nation I have seen. Their style is not, as on the British instruments to which we are accustomed, deliberate and solemn, but quick and lively; nevertheless the sound is smooth and pleasant. It is remarkable that, with such rapid fingerwork, the musical rhythm is maintained and that, by unfailingly disciplined art, the integrity of the tune is fully preserved through the ornate rhythms and the profusely intricate polyphony – and with such smooth rapidity, such unequal quality, such discordant concord. . . . They introduce and leave rhythmic motifs so subtly, they play the tinkling sounds on the thinner strings above the sustained sound of the thicker strings so freely, they take such secret delight and caress (the strings) so sensuously, that the greater part of their art seems to lie in veiling it, as if 'that which concealed is bettered – art revealed is art shamed.'
>
> Thus it happens that those things which bring private and ineffable delight to a people of subtle appreciation and sharp discernment, burden rather than delight the ears of those who, in spite of looking do not see and in spite of hearing do not understand; to unwilling listeners, fastidious things appear tedious and have a confused and disordered sound.

This has a curiously contemporary feel; people, after all, are still complaining of Irish music that it 'all sounds the same', that it is tedious and disordered.

Giraldus' remarks were echoed some six hundred years later by Edward Bunting, who noted down the performances at the Belfast Harp Festival of 1792:

> ... all the Melodies played by the harpers were performed with so much quickness that they did not bear the least comparison with the manner in which he had been accustomed to hear them played on the flute, violin, etc., by the Professors of those instruments, who usually performed them so slow that the melody was nearly lost, and they were sung by the better class of people in the same drawling sleepy style.

Bunting was witness to a tradition that was on its last legs; only one of the harpers, Denis Hempson of Magilligan, used the old finger-nail technique (the others using the modern method of playing with the flesh of the finger). By the 1820s the old harp was gone forever.

*Denis Hempson or O'Hempsey*

The harp is not regarded as a traditional instrument by traditional musicians; it was hardly a folk instrument anyway, since in its heyday it depended on an elaborate system of aristocratic patronage. Since modern performers on the harp can have no really accurate idea of how the old harp was played, they use, *faute de mieux*, a technique which is by and large classical. One can safely assume, for instance, that the harp-playing of Derek Bell bears little relation to what Cambrensis, or even Bunting, heard; neither does it accord to traditional practice on other instruments. Granted, there are those who play dance music on the harp; the result, however, is 'confused and disordered' to many ears. If the harp is a symbol of Ireland, it is an Ireland that finds itself uncomfortably balancing between two stools.

## The Bodhrán

The bodhrán is a shallow, one-sided drum of a type found in many cultures throughout the world. Its use in modern traditional music is mainly due to its adoption by the late Seán Ó Riada, who preferred it, in his arrangements for Ceoltóirí Cualann (latterly the Chieftains), to the snare-drums used in *ceílí* bands. Previously it was associated with the annual forays of the Mummers or Wren-Boys, who used it to make a lot of noise – the Irish word *bodhrán* means 'deaf thing' or 'deafener'. The noise was sometimes accentuated by the addition of tambourine-style jingles to the rim, and the bodhrán is sometimes called a tambourine in some parts of the country. Indeed, it has been suggested that *bodhrán* is a corruption of *'bourine.*

The skin most commonly used for the head of the bodhrán is goat; calf and even greyhound skin is also used, and it was reliably reported that a ring of greyhound procurers existed in Dublin some years ago. There are also several semi-apocryphal stories of lads ruining potential bodhráns by hunting them with shotguns or, on at least one occasion, a machine-gun. Some commentators find poetic justice in these anecdotes.

Ó Riada's elevation of the bodhrán to the status of a musical instrument found approval in many quarters; however, it is only fair to say that many musicians regard it with derision, or, at best, suspicion. The late Seamus Ennis, when asked how to play a bodhrán, replied, 'With a penknife.' There are reasons for this attitude. The bodhrán seems easy to play; to the non-musician who wants to be thought of as a musician the bodhrán seems an easily-acquired passport into a select company. Or it may be that he perceives the music as an entertainment which everyone may, or should, join in. Whatever the motivation, the results are sometimes execrable: a piano accordion, for example, accompanied by a battery of four or five aspiring bodhrán players, all producing personal variations on what they think is the beat, is hardly likely to be music. On the other hand, the bodhrán can give good 'lift' to a session or to solo playing. The combination of flute and drum is a well-tried one, and many flute-players actively like a good bodhrán accompaniment.

The bodhrán is played with a stick or with the hand. The stick can vary considerably in shape and dimensions: some players prefer to use one end of the stick, some like a leather loop on the stick, some like a big stick and others like a wee stick. Playing with the hand involves a rocking motion between the thumb or ball of the thumb and the fingers or outside edge of the palm. Since the drum is open-ended, various shifts of timbre and pitch can be achieved by manipulating the hand, fingers, or arm on the inside of the skin, and some virtuoso players, notably Johnny McDonnagh of De Danann, have developed this technique to a very high level: the melodic line of a tune can be followed or counterpointed. Some players also vary the sound by playing a few bars on the wooden rim of the bodhrán, or on the studs which hold the skin in place. The effect, at times, is not unlike a machine-gun, and if you are not prepared for it, it can be very bad for the nerves. In group playing, the bodhrán – inspired, perhaps, by the example of jazz drummers – sometimes takes a solo. This can be good crack but is not to be generally recommended except among consenting adults.

### *How To Play The Bodhrán*

If you really want to play the bodhrán, it would do no harm to observe the following guidelines:

Familiarise yourself as thoroughly as possible with the music before approaching within smelling distance of a goat-skin. If you can, learn some other instrument besides the bodhrán. At the very least, you should be able to lilt a selection of about fifty tunes in varying tempos.

If you want to join in a session, ask the other musicians first, or wait until you are asked. This common courtesy should be observed by all musicians, but bodhrán players seem to ignore it more than most.

If there is already a bodhrán player in the session, forget about it.

If, after the requisite amount of hard work and sensitive listening, your playing is acceptable to other musicians don't be afraid to express yourself. The obverse of the ignorant and insensitive is the paranoiac and guilt-ridden player who cannot enjoy himself for fear of spoiling others' enjoyment. If you must play the bodhrán, then play it.

# Other Instruments

## Miscellaneous Stringed Instruments

In recent years a whole family of stringed instruments have been utilised in traditional music: these include the mandoline, the mandocello, the bouzouki, the cittern, the tenor-banjo and the banjo-mandoline. Generally these are tuned like a fiddle, or tuned to an open D or G chord, and played with a plectrum. They may be used for accompaniment or for melody. While somewhat inflexible in tone, they can generate an exciting rhythmical impact. Having said that, there is suspicion in some quarters that handlers of these instruments are really failed fiddlers; on the other hand, many fiddlers or fluters enjoy a bouzouki accompaniment.

The guitar is a different story. Until recently it was completely outside the traditional pale and was associated almost exclusively with so-called 'ballad' groups such as the Clancy Brothers or the Wolfe Tones. However, the folk boom of the sixties and seventies led some musicians to experiment with the possibility of playing reels and jigs on the guitar, with varying degrees of success. The trouble with the guitar is that the finger-picking style laboriously cultivated by some folk players is not really suitable for the very fast incisive rhythms of Irish traditional music; so, a John Renbourne or a Pierre Bensusan may make nice music by interpreting an Irish jig on the guitar, but it will not be traditional music; the rhythms will have to be significantly altered to accommodate the style. A more appropriate strategy is to treat the guitar somewhat like a tenor banjo, and use a plectrum. While this style of playing ignores many of the inherent characteristics of the instrument, it is better suited to the music, and players like Paul Brady (before his incursions into rock music) and Arty McGlynn have succeeded in making the guitar accommodate the full range of traditional expression. Very few other guitarists, however, have this kind of technical brilliance.

## The Piano

The use of the piano in traditional music is questionable, though many older musicians actively seek a piano accompaniment. It is possible to trace its presence in the music back to the early recordings of Irish music made in America and its subsequent use in *céilí* bands; one could also speculate about the piano's representing an ideal of musical respectability. One of the problems is that the piano's predetermined intonation sometimes clashes with that of more 'traditional' instruments; the other is that many piano 'drivers', as they are sometimes known, are insensitive and domineering. However, there are some players, notably Charlie Lennon, who are content to accompany the music instead of drowning it in a sequence of inappropriate chords; significantly, Charlie Lennon is perhaps better known as a fiddle-player.

## The Hammer Dulcimer

The origins of this instrument are obscure; several versions of it exist in many different musical cultures, notably in the Arab world. It consists of an open trapezium-shaped sounding board strung with piano wire or similar material; the 'hammers' are generally two lengths of wood or wire with a spoon-shaped head sometimes wrapped in wool. These are held in the hand and used to strike the appropriate string-course. The most renowned player in recent years was the late John Rea of Glenarm, Co. Antrim.

The hammer dulcimer can sometimes sound strange when played with other instruments, or, for that matter, by itself; since it has no damping mechanism, notes will be sustained beyond their useful duration, and interfere with the notes that are actually struck at any given time.

Derek Bell of the Chieftains has latterly brought the instrument to the attention of an uncomprehending public, calling it a 'tiompán' (an obscure and conjectural medieval Irish instrument) which in all likelihood it is not.

### The Bones

Perhaps this item should have been included under 'The Bodhrán', since many bodhrán players are bone players, and vice versa. Both fulfill similar functions: to provide a rhythmic accompanying noise. The bones in question are usually two cow-ribs which have been boiled and dried, though I notice that an English supplier of folk instruments is advertising 'bones' made of mahogany; perhaps this is in deference to the Animals' Rights movement.

The bones are held in the hand and used like castanets.

### The Spoons

The spoons are a similar class of animal. Ordinary kitchen spoons – whether soup spoons or dessert spoons – seem quite adequate for the job, though many fanatical spoons players will go to inordinate lengths to get weapons of the right material, weight, and resonance; the handles, similarly, will be customized by paring with files and wrapping with various kinds of tape. The spoons are played by gripping them between the fingers of one hand and beating them against an object such as the other hand, the knees, the table, or, as I have witnessed on several occasions, armpits, shoes, and other people's heads. Spoons players are to be admired for their resourcefulness: should their instruments happen to be mislaid, or stolen, they will resort to clicking two bottles together or rattling a handful of loose change; unhappily, decimal coinage has not got the same satisfying ring as the old copper pennies.

## Dancing and Music

Irish instrumental music is, by and large, dance music; or at least it was until comparatively recently. Now, with the exception of a few isolated pockets in areas such as Clare, West Cork and Kerry, it is a listening music, notwithstanding the vestigial audience participation – bodhrán-beating, bottle-clicking, coin-rattling and hand-clapping – often witnessed at fleadhanna cheoil and informal sessions.

> Dancing is very general among the poor people. Almost universal in every cabbin. Dancing-masters of their own rank travel through the country from cabbin to cabbin, with a piper or blind fiddler; and the pay is six pence a quarter. It is an absolute system of education. Weddings are always celebrated with much dancing.
>
> Arthur Young
> *A Tour in Ireland* (1776-1779)
>
> Music and dancing being in fact as dependent the one on the other as cause and effect, it requires little or no argument to prove that the Irish, who are so sensitively alive to the one, should excel in the other. Nobody, unless one who has seen and also *felt* it, can conceive the inexplicable exhilaration of the heart which a dance communicates to the peasantry of Ireland.
>
> Francis O'Neill
> *Irish Minstrels and Musicians* (1913)
>
> Anything more lugubrious than the drone of the pipe, or the jig danced to it, or the countenances of the dancers and musicians, I never saw. Round each set of dancers the people formed a ring; the toes went in, and the toes went out; then there came certain mystic figures of hands across and so forth. I never saw less grace or seemingly less enjoyment – no, not even in a quadrille.
>
> William Thackeray
> *Irish Sketch Book* (1843)

It is perhaps a tribute to the power and resilience of the music that it has survived the loss of its primary function; nevertheless, it must be a cause of some concern, or regret, that most musicians under the age of thirty have never played for a traditional dance – traditional, that is, as opposed to the kind of dancing promulgated by the various schools of dancing. Practised mainly by children bedecked in medals and pseudo-Celtic costumes, this activity, endowed with a set of rules of Kafkaesque complexity, exists solely for the purpose of competition. Its relation to music is minimal, as Breandán Breathnach pointed out:

> It is seriously urged in some quarters that the music used at competitions should be provided on pre-recorded tapes and played in strict dance tempo. Strict dance tempo is not playing strictly in time, as I thought when I first met the expression. It is the tempo which some body of adjudicators has decided to be the appropriate one for the dance in question. People from the schools frequently find themselves in difficulty when confronted with music played by untamed musicians.
> 'Dancing in Ireland', *Dal gCais* (1983)

An Irish Jig.

Most children educated in this discipline, are, in fact, incapable of lilting a tune, and are familiar only with the four or five tunes to which they have been programmed: these will have indeed been drilled into them by the medium of cassette tape on which the tunes – usually played by an accordionist of dubious musicality – are solemnly announced as 'A Beginner's Reel', 'An Advanced Reel', 'A More Advanced Reel', and so on. Perhaps one of the most telling reflections on this bizarre manifestation of Irish culture is that so many children, with the onset of puberty, become lapsed dancers.

The reasons for the demise of the traditional dance are many and varied. Unquestionably, the efforts of the Catholic clergy, who saw it as an occasion of sin, had something to do with the matter. As Francis O'Neill puts it in his *Irish Folk Music* (1910):

> Traditional Irish music could have survived even the disasters of the Famine had not the means for its preservation and perpetuation – the crossroads and farmhouse dances – been capriciously and arbitrarily suppressed. 'Twas done in my native parish of Caherea, West Carberry, in my boyhood days, by a gloomy puritanical pastor. And the

---

### The Curate and the Goat

Barron – a dancing master from West Limerick – was holding his classes in Jimmo Sexton's house, near Mullagh. The local curate rode out from Mullagh fully intending to scatter the dancing school. When he came into the house he found Barron on the floor putting a pupil through his paces while the music was supplied by a concertina player. The priest grabbed the concertina, flung it on the fire and put his boot on it. Then he turned to Barron and is reported to have said: 'Clear out of here, you dancin' devil, or I'll make a goat of you.' To which Barron retorted, 'If you do I'll give you a *púcán* up the arse with my two horns.' Pat Barron did not evacuate Mullagh because the curate wanted him out; instead he resumed his classes and remained for another year or so; and he didn't turn into a goat as far as I know.

Junior Crehan, fiddle player,
quoted in *Dal gCais* (1977)

same senseless hostility to Irish music and pastimes was drastically enforced with a whip wielded by a PP on the backs of my nephews and their fellow revivalists...

Such was the attitude of the Church until well into this century; now Irish dancing, at least of the school variety, has come to embody a clerical ideal of Catholic purity, a stance against the wilder excesses of the jitterbug, the Twist, the Pogo-dance, or whatever manifestation of commercial culture is in vogue at the time: so much so, that Mass-goers are now treated to the spectacle of costumed teams of youngsters jigging in the aisles.

There are, however, some signs of hope for the traditional set dances, as young (post-pubertal) people in several urban centres have embarked on an enthusiastic revival under the guidance of such inspired teachers as Joe O'Donovan of Cork. Let us hope they escape the codification and the obsession with bureaucracy which has plagued competitive dancing.

## The Song Tradition

> The mode of reciting ballads (on Inisheer) is singularly harsh. I fell in with a curious man today beyond the east village, and we wandered out on the rocks towards the sea. A wintry shower came on while we were together, and we crouched down in the bracken, under a loose wall. When we had gone through the usual topics he asked me if I was fond of songs, and began singing to show me what he could do.
>
> The music was much like what I have heard before on the islands – a monotonous chant with pauses on the high and low notes to mark the rhythm; but the harsh nasal tone in which he sang was almost intolerable. His performance reminded me in general effect of a chant I once heard from a party of Orientals I was travelling with in a third-class carriage from Paris to Dieppe...
>
> J. M. Synge *The Aran Islands*

To generalise about the Irish song tradition – or even, perhaps, to *call* it the 'Irish' song tradition – is difficult. There are obvious stylistic parallels between some Irish vocal techniques and those of, say, Western Scotland (whether it be Presbyterian hymn singing or a Catholic song of unrequited love); the 'high lonesome' style of the Appalachian mountains is not a million miles away, emotionally and technically, from that of some Donegal singers; and it has become fashionable, in recent years, to suggest links between Eastern and Irish music:

> In the area of vocal ornamentation East and West come close. I once played a Claddagh recording of Máire Áine [Ni Dhonncha] singing 'Barr an tSléibhe' for an Indian Professor of music who refused to believe, until I showed her the sleeve of the record, that it was an Irish song. She claimed, and demonstrated by singing to me, that the song bore a strange resemblance to an Indian (North) raga about a young girl being lured toward a mountain. The Professor was interested in the mode, the pitching of the voice, and certain notes which were characteristic of both the raga and 'Barr an tSléibhe'.
> 
> Fanny Feehan, 'Suggested Links Between Eastern and Celtic Music' in *The Celtic Consciousness* ed. Robert O'Driscoll (1982)

If Ireland is part of a wider cultural community, Ireland itself contains differing communities. It is likely that a particular community will have built up a repertory of song from very diverse sources, on a wide range of topics: songs of love, unrequited love, emigration, war, drinking, soldiers, sailors, tinkers, tailors; music-hall songs, blackface minstrel songs, classic 'Child' ballads, songs written in praise of the locality, hedge-school compositions with intricate and absurd rhyme-schemes, nonsense songs; songs of English, Irish or Scottish origin, as recognised by the title of Hugh Shields' exemplary study of the song tradition of Magilligan in North Derry, *Shamrock, Rose and Thistle:*

> Oh, a stream like crystal it runs down, it's rare for to be seen,
> Where there you'll see the Irish oak trimmed with the ivy green;
> The shamrock, rose and thistle and the lily too beside
> They do flourish all together, boys, along the Faughan side.

The tradition, in other words, is not static, nor is it confined to one genre. A distinction is often made between so-called *sean-nós* singing in Irish and singing in English; yet the singer of the 'big' songs in Irish may often include all of the above material in his repertory. In a night's singing in the village of Coolea in the West Cork Gaeltacht, for instance, you will hear elaborately-ornamented songs which might indeed remind one of a North Indian raga; chorus drinking songs, sporting songs, songs from the classic ballad repertory, and newly-composed songs on local incidents – like the coming of the ESB to Coolea:

> Oh Johnny dear and did you hear what all the neighbours say?
> For the ESB with 'lectricity is landed in Coolea
> For to give us light by day or night with bulbs that do not blow
> Oh dear, oh dear, if we had them here some fifty years ago.

And in between a set or two might be danced, a story told, some drink consumed. The situation, in fact, might be the genre: a context which allows a varied emotional range, in which the music and singing is itself part of an ongoing conversation, a debate between the community and itself and the concerns of the wider world.

And of course, in other communities, sectarian or 'party' songs might be sung, though never, in my experience, to the exclusion of other material. In any case, Orange and Green might be mirror images of each other. As Hugh Shields puts it, 'party songs are culturally complementary: while expressing different allegiances they use similar themes, forms, styles and melodies. Customarily performed out of earshot of any whose religion they might offend, they can be compared with local topical songs whose malicious shafts of satire make them unsuitable for the ears of the targets selected on no sectarian basis. Jimmy McCurry, the fiddler from Myroe, composed such songs: though he was a Presbyterian, his songs have a diversity of "Gaelic" features such as are common in Anglo-Irish poetry and music as a whole.'

Neither is it uncommon for singers to have songs from both camps: possibly these are sung in a spirit of irony, or a desire to show that one knows the other side as well as one knows one's own; knowledge is power. Or perhaps they are sung because they are good songs.

Proinsias Ó Conluain's notes to Robert Cinnamond's record 'You Rambling Boys of Pleasure' extends this point:

> Robert Cinnamond's songs and ballads covered such a wide range of subjects that no one record could accommodate even a reasonably representative selection of them. Many of them were of historical or political or social interest. For example, he had a great number of songs dealing with the rising of 1798, and one of his favourites was 'I Am A Bold United Man,' about the fisherman who hung his net upon a tree and followed Henry Joy McCracken. 'That's the best one I have about the Antrim men of '98', he said, but he had most of the well-known songs of the period and to some, like 'Betsey Gray' and 'Lord Edward Fitzgerald', he put a tune of his own.
>
> He had numerous ballads dealing with the sectarian affrays in the north of Ireland in the last century and he sang those he fancied, whichever side of the political and religious divide they came from. For example, he would sing the Orange 'Dolly's Brae', about a fight near Castlewellan in Co. Down in 1849, but he also had a version of events as seen from the Roman Catholic side – something which has not survived otherwise in ballad tradition. On this record he sings the Orange song, 'The Aghalee Heroes' – Aghalee is not far from his native place – but he also had ballads in which the Orangemen were anything but heroes, e.g. 'The Chapel Hill Fight' (at Glenavy) and 'The Battle of Glenoe' (Co. Tyrone). Both these incidents, involving provocative Orange marches through Roman Catholic areas, occurred around the 12th of July, 1829, the year of Catholic Emancipation, and it is safe to say that Robert Cinnamond was the one man in Ireland who still remembered the ballad accounts in 1966, when he recorded them for Radio Telefis Eireann. Some say that these sectarian ballads would be as well forgotten; yet they are the very stuff (unfortunately) of Ulster history in the last century and go a long way to explaining the continuing conflicts of today.

## Some Notes on *Sean-Nós*

*Sean-nós* literally means 'old-style'. In the context of traditional performance, it is often applied to the singing, in Irish, of the *Gaeltachtaí* (or Irish-speaking areas) of the west of Ireland. There are difficulties with the term: whether it was invented by the Gaelic League to distinguish the musical expression of 'a language which the stranger does not know', or whether it is an indigenous expression, is open to some question; certainly, it seems unlikely that native Irish speakers would use the term to describe a native form of singing. Again, there are clear differences (and, granted, parallels) between the singing of the Donegal Gaeltacht and that of Coolea in Munster; should *sean-nós* include them both? Ironically, most singing in Irish, as promulgated by members of the Gaelic League and by Feiseanna Cheoil (Music Festivals), is not what is usually understood by *sean-nós*; nor does it accord to any perception of the notion of 'traditional'. Yet the word *sean-nós* has become a shibboleth, and many *Gaeilgeoirí* (Irish language enthusiasts) go so far as to maintain the patently absurd conclusion that no musician can be a traditional musician without an understanding of the *sean-nós*; others take the converse position, that everything is Irish – and therefore traditional – if expressed in the Irish language.

All these notions ignore the fact that, for better or worse, English is the language of the vast majority of traditional singers in Ireland, and singing in both languages shares many common features. Further, many aficionados of the *sean-nós* school of thought would be surprised to find that Joseph Taylor, recorded by Percy Grainger in Lincolnshire in the early years of this century, used vocal techniques which would be familiar to a Connemara singer.

Despite its inadequacies, the term *sean-nós* may be a useful one if it means those characteristics which distinguish traditional singing from classical singing. (Some academics prefer the term 'folk' to 'traditional' singing. Yet, in Ireland, a 'folk singer' usually refers to a performer of the Wolfe Tone or Clancy Brothers type.) As I have suggested, Irish traditional singing contains several different idioms; yet all Irish traditional singing can be contrasted to that of the European concert platform tradition.

Traditional singers, for example, do not employ dramatic effects to illustrate the emotional content of a song: rolling of the eyes, gesticulations of the hands, smiles and frowns are inappropriate, as are the use of crescendo or diminuendo. Because of this, many observers of traditional singing have called it impersonal; perhaps 'understated' is better, since the utterance of a traditional singer is, in fact, very personal in that the performance is his alone, and recognised as being so. It is just that the dimensions in which he operates are different. The so-called trained voice of the opera singer would be counter-productive to a traditional singer: its intentional volume and vibrato would tend to diminish any of the subtler effects used by him. The singing of the late Tom Pháidín Tom of Carna, Connemara, is a case in point. By classical standards, the voice hardly exists: it sounds, on record, like a conversational whisper; yet this is beautiful and complex singing, in which a slight change of rhythm, an almost unquantifiable pause, can make a world of difference to one's perception of the song.

It has been said that this kind of singing gains its effects by melodic decoration; but it is important to remember that the traditional singer does not conceive of ornament, or melodic variation, as being conceptually different to the melody itself. The song is the way it is sung; since there is no absolute melody, one is free to interpret it as one wishes; the song is the totality of the effects that may be deployed at any one time.

Similarly, the mode of performance is different. The traditional singer usually sings sitting down; he may not even face his audience. If he happens to be holding a cup of tea or a glass in his hand when he is asked to sing he may go on doing so. This is not to say that the performance is casual; his agreeing to sing, for instance, may be the culmination of a very structured series of requests and denials. One might go so far as to say that knowing when to sing (and what to sing) is a significant element in the singer's art. The song, after all, is one expression of whatever is going on at that particular social gathering. At critical emotional points in the song a member of the company may grasp the singer's hand and wind it rhythmically; knowing when and how to do this is also, possibly, an art of its own.

I was present once at a gathering in Carna, Co. Galway, held to celebrate the fact that one of the locals had won the annual Galway hooker regatta. The venue was one of those enormous plastic lounge bars that have blossomed all over the West of Ireland in recent years. The place was crammed to the doors. The conversation was mainly in Irish; there were also snippets of English, American, German, Dutch, even

Scottish Gaelic; and through this multilingual hubbub one could hear, at one point in the night, a girl singing. She was sitting in one corner surrounded by a tiny knot of listeners, an island of rapt attention, oblivious to the rest of the world. A woman grasped one of her hands, a man the other. The singer's eyes were closed; the whole thing had the air of a trance, of an archaic ritual that was intensely concerned with the moment, the present, the here-and-now; the song itself was somehow of the situation:

Sneachta séite is é a shíor-chur ar Shliabh Uí Fhloinn
Is tá mo ghrá-sa mar bláth na n-áirní ar an droighneán donn. . .

(Blown snow falls forever on O'Flynn's mountain
And my love is like the sloe-blossom on the blackthorn tree. . .)

However, one does not have to be there to appreciate the depth and the integrity of this kind of singing, and fortunately some very fine examples — though nowhere near enough — are preserved on record. Many traditional singers, in fact, have been recorded more through accident than design, and a comprehensive document of this complex art still remains to be made.

## Recent Developments

Since Irish traditional music depends on an individualistic embellishment of the melodic line, it is often held that it is heard to best effect in solo performances. This may be. Nevertheless, musicians have always played along with other musicians, for company, for crack, for the 'lift' that another musician will give to your own playing, or maybe simply to create a bigger sound for dancing to. In these circumstances the musicians will have to arrive at some implicit (or explicit) agreement to stay within certain limits of ornamentation and melodic variation; this kind of conversation is often as satisfying as solo playing.

The first readily-identifiable group arrangement was known as the céilí band. It has been suggested that the céilí band was an invention of the late Seamus Clandillon of Radio Station 2RN, the precursor of Radio Éireann (now RTE), in the late 1920s; however, it is likely that similar groups would

have existed before then, and the Kilfenora Céilí
Band is thought to have been founded in 1907 (*see*
'The Traditional Music of County Clare' by Séamus
Mac Mathúna, *Treoir* vol. 9 no. 6). Whatever the case,
the céilí band seemed to fulfil the kind of role later
adopted by the showbands of the early sixties – that
is, playing for public dances – and each band soon
built up its own crowd of devotees, or fans. The céilí
band competitions in the *fleadhanna* of the fifties, in
fact, generated some of the excitement and partisan-
ship of All-Ireland football and hurling finals, and
still attract the biggest attendance of any competi-

tion, despite the fact that the bands' primary function – playing for dances – has receded significantly.

The line-up for a céilí band varied considerably: a typical traditionally-based band might include three fiddles, two flutes, a button accordion, drums and piano; others, orientated towards a more urban audience – in Irish centres in London and New York, for example – might add saxophones, a double bass, even trombones, usually played by non-traditional session musicians who read from a score. These latter arrangements were hardly born of musical necessity; they were a reflection of the uncertain social status of traditional music in the eyes of many, and as a hybrid of two musical languages it is possible that they ended up expressing neither.

Seán Ó Riada, in a 1962 radio broadcast, damned céilí bands as making 'a rhythmic but meaningless noise with as much relationship to music as the buzzing of a bluebottle in an upturned jamjar'. This was fair comment in some instances; in others, myopic. Bands like the Kilfenora and the Tulla had a great sense of rhythm; you could feel the joy in their playing, and they were great for dancing to. Because there were no formal arrangements of the kind later introduced by Ó Riada, there were no inhibitions, and the individual musician could treat the tune as he liked, so long as he kept within implicit limits of decoration and timing. The informed listener could identify these individual nuances, ignoring, if he wished, the sometimes unnecessary piano and drums accompaniment.

Ó Riada's own development of the group concept of playing coincided with the so-called traditional music 'revival' of the sixties. The movement has been attributed to many factors, and a detailed examination of its whys, wherefores and whereabouts is impossible here. Certainly, the influence of the early *fleadhanna cheoil,* instigated by Comhaltas Ceoltóirí Éireann in the fifties, is undeniable, as is that of 'ballad' groups like the Clancy Brothers and The Dubliners. But it also seems to have been part of a wider cultural phenomenon which, for the urban young, would have included such diverse characters as Bob Dylan, Joan Baez, Woody Guthrie, Ewan McColl, Bert Lloyd, the Watersons, Bert Jansch, the Incredible String Band, Bob Davenport, Blind Lemon Jefferson, Blind Willie Johnson and Blind Boy Fuller, to name a few.

At any rate, it was a time for experiment. In what seemed then to be a radical gesture, Ó Riada proposed a concept of group playing which he thought emphasised 'the essentially solo effect' of the music. His 'Ceoltóirí Cualann' were organised with something of the discipline of a chamber ensemble. Solo playing was interspersed with bursts of duets, trios, quartets, or whatever, providing melodic and thematic variations – in fact, for possibly the first time, the integrity of the old dance music forms, the jigs and the reels, was broken; the tune, in Ó Riada's hands could now be dissected into various motifs; harmony was allowable. While most traditional musicians viewed these developments with some suspicion, they were acclaimed by a wider audience, and a music until now confined to parish halls and the back rooms of private and public houses suddenly became respectable; adulatory notices appeared in the *Irish Times*. For many, it was almost as if traditional music had been reborn, or, indeed, had never existed before. Yet Ó Riada's practice and preaching had its contradictions: he castigated the use of the piano, only to replace it with a harpsichord (thinking it might sound like the old Irish harp); he recognised the artistic depth of the *sean-nós* tradition, and then made considerable use of the Irish tenor Seán Ó Sé; he banned drums, and brought in the bodhrán; and many of his arrangements tended towards the classical European music whose influence on the native tradition he so much deplored.

Ceoltóirí Cualann became the Chieftains; other groups such as Planxty and the Bothy Band followed; the music reached an international audience, and many musicians now in their thirties would trace their early influences back to that period. Ironically, many of them found themselves returning to the raw material from which Ó Riada moulded his aesthetic, rather like the movement from the pan loaf back to wholemeal and the wheaten farl. Others persisted in tinkering with the basic structures of the music, most noticeably when their traditional experience was minimal (Horslips, for example); bastardised genres like 'folk-rock' were announced as inspired creative achievements.

'Innovation' of this kind is still with us – the composer Shaun Davey, for example, has earned some popular, if not critical, acclaim for his mixed marriage of uilleann pipes and film score music.

One would suspect, however, that the really innovative music is practised by those who recognise the depth and complexity of the tradition itself. To know the way forward you must also know the way back.

## Etiquette

To the casual observer, a pub session of traditional music may appear haphazard and undisciplined: tunes are struck up at seemingly random intervals, for no discernible reason; some musicians may not join in at all, but may engage in conversational topics apparently unrelated to the music; and some punters (i.e. non-musicians) may, at unpredictable moments, utter inarticulate cries of what might be encouragement. The temptation is to think that any kind of behaviour is permissible. In reality, the session, like any form of social or artistic discourse, is governed by a complex set of implicit rules.

Students of ethnomusicology have been known to write theses on the matter; the purpose of the few brief notes that follow is merely to indicate a more or less proper code of behaviour for the punter.

## Tape-Recorders, Cameras

The uncritical use of the cassette tape-recorder is an increasingly widespread phenomenon, especially since micro-chip technology has enabled machines to be disguised as packets of cigarettes. Many musicians have reluctantly accepted their ubiquity. However, the good-mannered punter will always ask permission to record; this will be granted in most cases, since the musician will usually be overwhelmed by this act of common decency. But it should be remembered that letting the musician know he is being taped may have an inhibiting effect on the music: which means that many of the best recordings of sessions have been furtive, made by persons of an ill-mannered and acquisitive disposition. Since the act of recording implies futurity, such people may never enjoy the here-and-now; they are absorbed in the technology, not the moment. A pleasure constantly deferred is likely to remain always out of reach.

Similar criteria apply to the use of the camera, especially flash, which is usually the only practical method in dark and smoke-infested pubs. The camera is an invasion of privacy. If you must photograph people, ask their permission. And having photographed them, arrange to send them copies.

Photographic or recording sessions which have been deliberately arranged for archival purposes are, of course, a different matter. But here also the rules of common decency – to treat musicians like human beings instead of objects – apply.

## Applause

Applause is a way of registering approbation or approval. At informal sessions of traditional music it may take many forms – from exhibitionistic whoops and gulders to a minimalist, barely-uttered 'good man yourself'. Normal hand-clapping may be appropriate, though it is rarely as prolonged as it would be at, say, a recital of classical music. The punter, after all, is not applauding his own good taste.

The inexperienced punter may be somewhat disconcerted by the custom whereby little whoops and screams are uttered while the music is in progress. These expressions of appreciation may not be as random as they seem. An attentive punter may, for example, make a little yelp at that point where the tune has been played once and is now about to be played again (tunes are played at least twice round), indicating (a) that he knows where a tune ends and (b) that he would like to hear it again, which he will anyway. On the other hand, the yelp may come at a point in the tune which is determined by the punter's perception of a particularly fine melodic variation; to the musician who just played it, it may have been a mistake. Or it may not.

That these usages are sanctioned by antiquity can be seen from the following excerpt from a 19th-century guide to ball-room etiquette:

> No person during a Country Dance should hiss, clap, or make any other noise, to interrupt the good order of the company. Snapping the fingers, in Country Dancing and Reels and the sudden howl or yell too frequently practised, ought particularly to be avoided, as partaking too much of the customs of barbarous nations. . . .

It will be readily observed that the practice of these gestures may be hazardous and liable to misinterpretation. The inexperienced punter will be relieved to hear that there is at least one cast-iron, unambiguous way of registering approval: that is, to buy the musicians drink.

The most convenient and correct way of achieving this is not to ask the musicians what they are having, but to get the barman to set them up a round. The barman will then indicate that the round was bought by 'the boy up at the bar' (where 'boy' means a person of either, or indeterminate sex). The musicians may acknowledge the gesture by raising their glasses, bows, flutes, or whatever; the punter will respond by raising his glass slightly, giving a barely-noticeable 'thumbs-up' sign, or the like. On no account should the impression be given that the punter has done the musicians a favour, or that they have become, by this mere commercial transaction, indebted to him.

This, by the way, is one of the few instances where one buys a drink for someone without any expectation of being bought one back. The round system in Ireland has many complex conventions which may shift according to geographical or temporal location, but it may be generally observed that if there is no such thing as a free lunch, there is no such thing as a free drink. People unaccustomed to the conventions (Germans, Americans, etc.) sometimes assume that the Irish are an incredibly generous nation who will, if you allow them, buy you drink all night. The reality may be that the Irish like to appear generous; the round system allows homage to be paid to the stereotype, while secretly acknowledging that everyone must stand his turn.

### Where to sit
This will depend, of course, on the design of the bar. However, it may be stated as a general rule that a punter should never sit in along with musicians, even though there may seem to be ample room. The odds are that an empty seat has been reserved for a musician who has not yet arrived, and may, indeed, not arrive at all. If you want to be in close proximity to the music, ask if that particular seat has been taken.

Bar acoustics are sometimes very peculiar, and it is often the case that the music can be heard to its best advantage if one is at some distance from it: for example, propped up against the bar counter. One can then talk, drink, and listen without causing a nuisance.

## Technical Supplement

### Pitch, Tuning, Intonation

> Whether or no a particular interval is appropriate to the musical context only the ear of the musician can decide.
> Ll. S. Lloyd *The Musical Ear*
>
> ... dissonance and consonance are attributes of human hearing, not qualities inherent in sound waves in the air.
> K. van Barthold, foreword to
> Ll. S. Lloyd and H. Boyle
> *Intervals, Scales and Temperaments*

There is no absolute 'being in tune'. It is a matter of the ear, of opinion, of musical and social agreement. Different cultures evolve different musical structures.

The Western classical scale is based on equal temperament, dictated by piano tuning: a compromise whereby every interval except the octave is deliberately slightly out of tune. The piano is a chromatic instrument. Chromaticism is inappropriate to traditional music.

Most traditional dance music is played in what we call, for convenience' sake, the keys of D and G. The bottom note in the scale of D is called D irrespective of the actual pitch of the instrument (which may be, in the case of the uilleann pipes, anything between B flat and E flat, depending on the instrument).

Certain notes in the scale, notably C and F, are variable: C, for example, may be anything from actual C up to C sharp, depending on the tune being played, or its position in the tune. These notes are sometimes slided.

Until comparatively recently, traditional music was not played in modern orchestral pitch (where A = 440 cycles per second). Even today, orchestral pitch is only taken as a vague general standard to which there are always exceptions: at the moment, it is fashionable in some circles to play half a tone above standard pitch (E flat) when the instrument can accommodate it; some fiddle players like to play a tone below pitch (C); and some uilleann pipes, as we have noted, may be pitched as low as B flat. In a session where several instruments are involved, the players will tune to the instrument with the least flexible pitch – the accordion, say, or the pipes or tin whistle.

To the classical ear, traditional playing often sounds 'out of tune'. Well, sometimes it may be, and sometimes not. But the odds are that an older traditional player (whose intonation may sound the strangest) will be perfectly in tune according to his own system.

Anyway, even classical players will sound out of tune to other classical musicians, as the following incident – recounted in Ll. S. Lloyd and H. Boyle's *Intervals, Scales and Temperaments* – demonstrates:

> Casals. . . took endless trouble in re-training the aural sense and habitual finger placement of students who, since childhood, had unquestioningly applied piano intonation to their stringed instruments. 'The effects of any neglect of this kind at the beginning of studies. . . can affect a player through the whole of his career, however gifted he may be.' I once met the living proof of this statement in a cellist who was attending Casals' Berkeley classes – a performer not without talent but who early on had been brainwashed by equal temperament. Hearing Casals for the first time, she exclaimed, 'He is *sooooo* beautiful – but why does he play out of tune?'

Similarly, people who complain that traditional music is out of tune usually turn out to be brainwashed by conventional music education.

To my ear, Donegal fiddle playing always sounds sharp. But the system is consistent, and it works.

Similarly, in traditional singing, there is no notion of a fixed pitch. A singer will sing in whatever pitch he happens to find convenient at the time. The classical idea of a bass voice, a tenor voice, a soprano voice, and so on, is not relevant to traditional music. A singer may change his pitch quite considerably from performance to performance, depending on the circumstances: his mood, the time of day, wherever he happens to be.

Having said that, a lot of traditional singers tend to pitch their voices as high as possible; this is deliberate. The tension is important. I think that possibly it is easier to produce the kind of fast ornament required in some styles of traditional singing if the voice is pitched very high.

A transcription of a traditional song written in, say, the key of B flat, does not mean that the song is in that key. It merely may have been sung in that pitch on one occasion. On other occasions, it may not be. It would be convenient if we were to adopt a convention of writing all traditional songs in one key, say G, with certain variable notes in that scale. Percy Grainger, who collected folk songs in England at the turn of the century, found that his singers employed 'one single loosely-knit modal folk-song scale', in which the third and seventh intervals were 'mutable and vague'. This applies equally well to Irish singing.

It cannot be said often enough that any classical training is disastrous to the traditional singer. Dr Richard Henebry stated the case uncompromisingly in his *Handbook of Irish Music* (1928). His use of the word 'instrument' here refers to harmonic composition based on equal temperament tuning, not the melodic line of Irish instrumental music:

> In the case of modern music the instrument has overrun everything and completely dominated and absorbed all vocal tradition. The modern educational stytem, which enforces on defenceless youngsters whatever fad happens to be uppermost at the time, to the exclusion of all others, has imposed this instrumental tradition everywhere, and, except the remnants in Ireland and a few out-of-the-way places like it, has completely destroyed the very memory of European human music. And those remnants are naturally 'out of tune', as one would expect from 'untaught peasants'. So children are taught the modern scale, and in punishment can never sing, nor hear human music more. And furthermore, in trying to sing their songs with fixed note places, they very rarely maintain the pitch, which is but an evidence of the protest of nature against artificial shackles, just as natural language is ever in protest against grammatical rules. Now, in regard to pitch, I think I can show some places in Irish music where it is maintained, as I believe it always is, with the greatest nicety, whereas the sagging bugbear in modern music is a result of the compromise nature is constantly forced to make with artificial tone places. . . and so complete is the dominance

of the instrument nowadays that instead of striving to imitate the voice, the voice is forced to imitate the instrument. Then the rich, red, warm colour of the human voice must yield to the white and dead tones of the modern opera singer. I knew some who did well in traditional singing until their success prompted them to take lessons in voice production from common modern teachers in towns, and they could never sing Irish any more. The colour was completely gone from the voice, and the power to glide and make complicated graces so dear to music.

The traditional singer or musician learns by ear, not by theory.

## Ornamentation

Irish traditional music is essentially melodic and its effects depend on the ornamentation, or embellishment, of the melodic line. Although the music has become more standardised in recent years, ornamentation will still vary from region to region, from person to person, from time to time. The traditional player will not use ornamentation in a consistent way in any given piece.

It may be also true to say that the traditional musician is not aware of ornamentation as being a separate constituent to the music itself: the tune is the totality of whatever different effects are employed at any one time. Many older traditional musicians may not use the terms detailed below, though these features may be present in their music. However, the terms have gained widespread acceptance in recent years, and it is useful at least to describe what is usually understood by them. In the absence of any comprehensive research into traditional musicians' own perception of what they are doing, it is difficult to establish a widely-accepted vocabulary to describe traditional techniques. I have heard the terms 'burl', 'hop', 'skip' and 'turn' used; but these might mean different things to different people.

The subject of ornamentation is a complex one and the following notes are intended only as a very general guide.

### *Grace note*

The single grace note is used to emphasise an accented note, or to separate two notes of the same pitch. The grace note is usually higher in pitch, but the exact note employed will vary: E, for example, may be graced by F, G, A, B or C, according to circumstances and the instrument used. Some musicians use a grace note *lower* in pitch than the accented note. Double grace notes usually take the form of *d e D, e f sharp E, f sharp g F sharp,* and so on.

*Roll*

The roll is a rhythmic device which sounds a bit like a hiccup. Basically, it consists of five movements: playing the note to be ornamented (the hop), then a note above it (the cut), then the hop, then a note below it (the tip), then the hop again. The exact manner in which this is done will depend on the instrument and the player. The notes played for the cut and the tip may vary considerably: a G roll, for example, may be played as *G a G f sharp G,* or *G b G e G*. The cut, and especially the tip, are the merest flicks of the finger, and cannot be written in conventional musical notation. Classical players reading a roll from the page will invariably get it wrong. I once spent several hours in the company of a traditional fiddle player who was showing a very accomplished jazz fiddler how to do a roll. At the end of the session he still hadn't got it – what put him out was the notion that the device existed outside of conventional time.

*Crann*

The Irish word *crann* means, among other things, a tree, a rod, a measure, a step in dancing. In traditional music, it refers to an ornament specifically associated with the uilleann pipes, though it is employed on other instruments such as the whistle, the flute, and even the fiddle (though I think it always sounds contrived on the fiddle). It consists of a kind of stuttering roll played on the D and E notes, in which no two grace notes are sounded consecutively.

# Where It's At

It is virtually impossible, and possibly undesirable, to give a comprehensive Michelin-type guide to traditional music venues. Ostensibly regular sessions in pubs may vanish like snow off a ditch once they are publicised in any coherent way; they may lapse anyway, for no better reason than the musicians' finding a more congenial venue. To some people, its comparative inaccessibility, its waywardness, its sometimes underground nature, are part of the charm of the music; others are exasperated by it. Occasional frustration is not necessarily a bad thing; an important

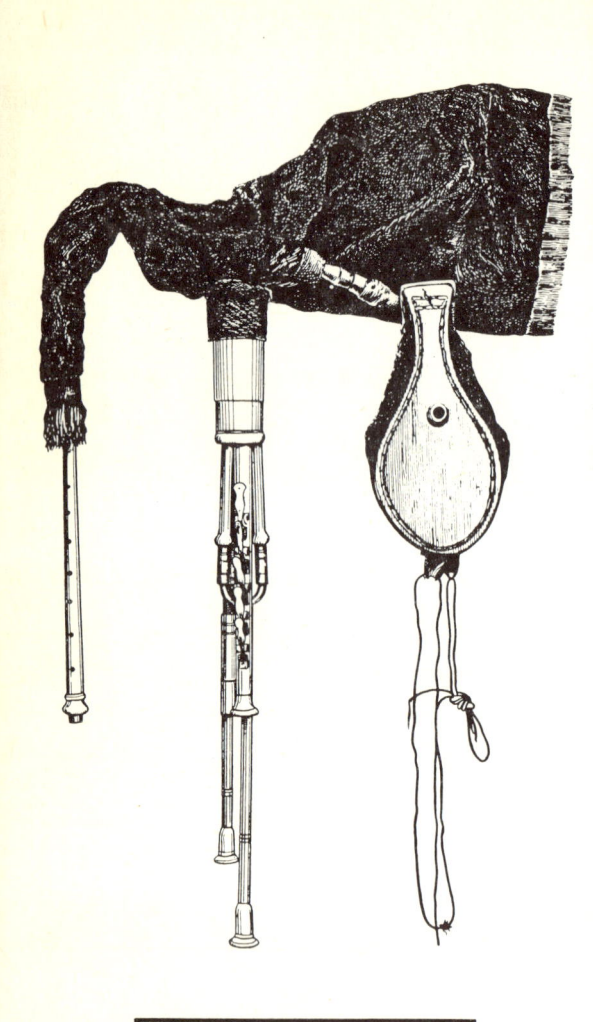

SET OF BAGPIPES, IVORY PIPES AND STOCK; MOUNTED ON GERMAN SILVER; FOUR DRONES — ONE WITH KEYS, CALLED A "REGULATOR." MADE PROBABLY ABOUT 1760 OR 1770. FROM THE DUCKETT COLLECTION, COUNTY CARLOW.

part of learning about music is finding it out for yourself, a process which may involve chance encounters on lonely mountain roads, complex negotiations of obscure verbal maps of neglected side-roads, crossroads, forks, hump-backed bridges and derelict garages; often, derelict pubs. The tourist in Ireland has only to ask and he will be directed towards something; whether or not it is what he thinks he is looking for is another matter.

Having said all that, one can acquire a modicum of almost reliable information by going to the local Tourist Board or by inquiring from Comhaltas Ceoltóirí Éireann, Belgrave Square, Monkstown, Co. Dublin, tel. Dublin 800295. The sessions to which one is directed may or may not be good in themselves – many of them, after all, will be geared towards tourist consumption – but one is bound to meet someone who knows where the 'real' action is.

Comhaltas will also provide a list of dates and venues for the annual *fleadhanna cheoil*. A *fleadh cheoil* means, literally, a 'feast of music'; this is quite possible. *Fleadhanna*, ostensibly, are competitions run along similar lines to the Gaelic football championship, with winners at county level proceeding to a provincial final, and hence to the All-Ireland final. For many punters and musicians, however, they provide an informal meeting place for exchange of tunes, news, views, and general crack; and indeed, *fleadhanna* were once, in the popular imagination, regarded as orgiastic occasions of unbridled alcoholism, sexuality and general mayhem. Some people say that things aren't what they used to be, but then nothing ever is. Those attending *fleadhanna* should know that the best music is often not to be found in the designated *fleadh* town or village but in a convenient backwater village; similarly, the best music may not be on the actual date of the occasion, but a day or two afterwards.

### *The Fiddle Competition*
There was this fiddle competition once upon a time.
And there were three fiddle players in for it.

The first fiddle player came up.
He was dressed in a dress suit.
He was wearing a white shirt and a dicky bow and he was carrying a crocodile-skin fiddle-case.

And when he brought out the fiddle,
what was it but a Stradivarius.
He started to play.
And beGod, he was useless.

The second fiddle-player came up.
He was dressed in a three-piece lounge suit
and a matching shirt and tie.
He had a nice mahogany fiddle-case and a good
    fiddle.
He rosined the bow and he drew it across the
    strings.
And beGod, *he* was useless.

So the third fiddle-player came up.
He had an ould battered shiny blue suit
and there was no collar to his shirt.
His toes were peeping out from his shoes.
And the fiddle-case
was held together with bits of string.
He brought out the fiddle,
and there was more strings on the fiddle
than there was on the bow.
He started to play.
And beGod, *he* was useless too.

>                    from the story-telling of
>                    Mick Hoy, fiddle-player.

# Selected Bibliography

## General
Breathnach, Breandán
*Folk Music and Dances of Ireland* (Mercier Press, 1971)
A cogent, if very occasionally misleading, introduction to the subject.

Henebry, Richard
*A Handbook of Irish Music* (Cork University Press, 1928)
An eccentric and sometimes bewildering analysis of the structure of the music; good chunks of entertaining and informative reading. Can be obtained through libraries.

O'Neill, Francis
*Irish Minstrels and Musicians*
*Irish Folk Music: A Fascinating Hobby* (both reprinted, E.P. Publishing, 1973)
The traditional flute-player Francis O'Neill was Superintendent of the Chicago Police Force at the turn of the century. These two important books contain very enjoyable anecdotal accounts of the music scene in Ireland and Chicago at the time, together with general histories of the subject.

Ó Canainn, Tomás
*Traditional Music in Ireland* (Routledge & Kegan Paul, 1978)
An account by a practising uilleann piper and singer; contains some interesting note-count analysis of tunes.

Ó Riada, Seán
*Our Musical Heritage* (Dolmen Press, 1982)
Edited transcripts of a series of radio programmes given by Ó Riada in 1962. Useful but surprisingly superficial in places; occasionally labouring under misapprehensions.

## Collections of Dance Music
Breathnach, Breandán
*Ceol Rinnce na h-Éireann, Cuideanna 1-3 (Dance Music of Ireland, Parts 1-3)* (Oifig an tSoláthair, Dublin, n.d.)
Music transcribed mostly from the playing of living musicians, and therefore containing a substantial amount of non-standard (i.e. not in O'Neill) settings. Essential.

Bulmer, D. R., and Sharpley, N.
*Music from Ireland, Vols. 1-4* (Celtic Music, Lincolnshire, 1974, 1976)
Contains a good number of tunes currently popular in sessions.

Krassen, Miles
*O'Neill's 'Music of Ireland': New and Revised Edition* (Oak Publications, New York, 1976)
This is O'Neill's 1850 tunes without the airs and the Carolan pieces, edited to conform to Krassen's notion of Michael Coleman's fiddle-playing; he sometimes ruins otherwise good settings.

Mitchell, Pat
*The Dance Music of Willie Clancy* (Mercier Press, 1976)
The only worthwhile book dealing with the style and repertoire of one musician. Very useful introductory chapter. Good tunes with variations as played at one specific sitting.

O'Neill, Francis
*The Dance Music of Ireland: 1001 Gems* (Walton's Ltd, Dublin, 1907)
Is it in The Book? This *is* The Book.

> As a corollary to the above, it is important to remember that many traditional musicians do not read music; nor do they find it necessary to do so. Any music learned from the above sources should always be done in conjunction to endless listening to traditional tunes as they are actually played: cold print cannot convey style; and style is often content. A book is only a book, and never to be trusted wholly.

**Songs**
Morton, Robin
*Come Day, Go Day, God Send Sunday* (Routledge & Kegan Paul, 1973)
An account of the life and times of the Fermanagh singer John Maguire. We need more of this sort of thing.

*Folk Songs Sung in Ulster* (Mercier Press, 1970)
Intended for more or less popular consumption, this book was chastised by some academics. It nevertheless contains some good songs.

Moulden, John
*Songs of the People, Part 1* (Blackstaff Press, 1979)
First part of an edition of the Sam Henry Collection (Henry published a folk-song column in the weekly Coleraine newspaper *The Northern Constitution* between 1923 and 1939). Moulden's stated aim of putting the songs back into singing circulation has already had repercussions.

Ó Muirithe, Diarmuid
*An t-Amhrán Macarónach* (An Clochomhar, Dublin, 1980)
An account, in Irish, of the macaronic (mixture of Irish and English) song tradition. Some incredible (and necessarily untranslateable) stuff. The song texts are unfortunately without airs.

Shields, Hugh
*Shamrock, Rose and Thistle: Folk Singing in North Derry* (Blackstaff Press, 1981)
This exemplary study cannot be praised highly enough. Should be bought, borrowed, or stolen, but preferably bought.

*A Short Bibliography of Irish Folk Song* (Folk Music Society of Ireland, n.d.)
Seems to contain just about everything on the subject.

Tunney, Paddy
*The Stone Fiddle: My Way to Traditional Song* (Gilbert Dalton, 1979)
Autobiography of the well-known traditional singer. Entertaining and occasionally mischievous; perhaps a personal extension of the hedge-school tradition? Contains a good number of song texts and airs.

Ó Lochlainn, Colm
*The Complete Irish Street Ballads* (Pan Books, 1984)
A reprint of the two-volume O Lochlainn collection. Great value; great songs.

O'Boyle, Sean
*The Irish Song Tradition* (Gilbert Dalton, 1976)
A misnomer, really: all the songs are from Ulster. Good songs with some rather eccentric introductory chapters.

**Miscellaneous**
Feldman, Allen and O'Doherty, Eamon
*The Northern Fiddler* (Blackstaff Press, 1979)
One of the few studies which attempt to relate trad-

itional music to a social and economic setting. Includes some great photographs, interviews with musicians (the one with the Tyrone fiddle-player John Loughran is especially good crack) and transcriptions of tunes.

Breathnach, Breandán
*Dancing in Ireland* (Dal gCais Publications, 1983)
This pamphlet appears to be one of the few useful accounts of the subject. Breathnach's succinct and occasionally acid style makes for entertaining reading.

Rimmer, Joan
*The Irish Harp* (Mercier Press, 1969)
Thorough and well-documented.

## Ten Recommended Records

Joe Cooley **Cooley** *Gael-Linn, CEF 044*
The late Joe Cooley played the accordion in the old 'press-and-draw' style; those who think that the instrument is necessarily inexpressive and insensitive should listen to Cooley's beautiful sense of rhythm, his lingering over the occasional wild note. Much of this recording was done at a pub session a few weeks before his death in December 1973; more than any high-tech studio operation, it captures the feel of the music, its capacity to express deep emotional ties. Utterly memorable.

Frankie Gavin **Up and Away** *Gael-Linn, CEF 103*
Frankie Gavin is more generally known as a fiddle-player and leader of *De Danann;* he is also a great flute-player. This album is an affectionate interpretation of the music of John McKenna, the Leitrim flute-player who made many influential 78s in the twenties; it is a perfect example of how the tradition operates, by constant personal shifts and re-definitions. Gavin plays it all with great skill, verve, and humour.

Tommy Potts **The Liffey Banks** *Ceirníní Cladaigh, CC13*
Some people would not classify this as traditional music at all. Potts is the lone wolf of Irish music; maybe his playing is a necessary corrective to the idea that the music only happens in sessions or groups. He takes the ornamental possibilities of a tune almost to their limit, using unfamiliar keys, classical-sounding modulations, and halting, off-beat rhythms which at times have only a notional connection with a dance-music structure. But an apprecia-

tion of what he is doing depends on knowing what he is changing; to play like this, you must be soaked in the tradition.

Seamus Tansey **The King of the Concert Flute** *Silver Hill, PSH 108*
Technically, this is a terrible recording; the flute can hardly be heard behind the otherwise excellent piano accompaniment of Charlie Lennon. But it's worth it for Tansey's absorption in his own technique, the moments of sheer joy. And after a while you forget the piano.

Robert Cinnamond **You Rambling Boys of Pleasure** *Topic, 12T269*
Those wishing to find an Ulster antecedent for the 'high-lonesome' singing of the Appalachians could well use this record as a set text. Cinnamond seems to pitch his voice as high as possible: the result is a constant, but always resolved, tension; a dialogue between the singer and the song. Ulster singing is generally regarded as comparatively unornamented; but what Cinnamond is doing, between subtle shifts of rhythm and pitch, is immense and complex. This is singing at its most committed.

Darach Ó Catháin **Darach Ó Catháin** *Gael-Linn, CEF 040*
Ó Catháin was raised in the tiny *Gaeltacht* of Rath Cairn in Meath; his singing is completely within the Connemara *sean-nós* tradition. His style has a kind of majestic assurance, a breadth of vision that can sometimes ignore ornamental possibilities for the sake of a long note, a sudden break in rhythm; and the ornaments, when they do happen, happen fast. The singing, at times, sounds relaxed, inevitable; yet he is always inventing. Having heard Ó Catháin's singing in other contexts, I feel that this record doesn't do him complete justice; it is, nevertheless, essential.

Mary Ann Carolan **Songs in the Irish Tradition** *Topic, 12 TS362*
The title is possibly a misnomer: some of the late Mrs Carolan's more ostensibly 'Irish' songs are ignored here for material which has close links with the English tradition. Great singing, nevertheless, done with calm authority, grace and humour. Listen to her 'Maid of Ballymore', one of the most apparently uneventful songs I've ever heard (young man meets beautiful girl, falls in love with her, asks her to marry

him, she agrees, they get the parents' consent, and live happily ever after). Somehow this becomes a great performance: her breath control, her phrasing, lead to a delicate tension you would never have suspected given the bare lyrics.

### Willie Clancy **The Minstrel from Clare** *Topic, 12T175*

Willie Clancy was one of the most influential musicians of the century. Like many men of his generation, he could not only play (mainly the uilleann pipes, also the fiddle, flute and tin whistle) but sing and dance and tell yarns as well: in this context, music was never mere technical accomplishment. Some of his warmth and humour comes over on this excellent record.

### Paddy Killoran **Back in Town** *Shanachie, 33003*

Killoran was one of the many musicians from the Sligo-Leitrim area who emigrated to the USA and recorded there in the twenties and thirties. His fiddle-playing has tended to be overshadowed by that of his contemporary, Michael Coleman; but many people prefer Killoran as the more 'traditional' of the two. Certainly, his playing, with its great bounce and drive, is rooted in the dance tradition; and he never lets the technique get in the way of the music.

### Noel Hill and Tony MacMahon **I gCnoc Na Graí** *Gael-Linn, CEF 114*

Why does it still seem a radical concept to record the music in the context in which it is played? Here Tony MacMahon, who was responsible for the Joe Cooley album, teams up with Noel Hill and a squad of set-dancers in Dan Connell's pub in Knocknagree, Co. Kerry. The great accordion and concertina playing is enhanced because it fulfills its primary function. This record is manifestly about something; we need to be reminded more often that music does not exist in a vacuum.